The Urban Gardener Indoors

The
Urban Gardener
Indoors

HOW TO GROW THINGS SUCCESSFULLY IN YOUR HOUSE, APARTMENT, OR CONDO

Sonia Day

KEY PORTER BOOKS

National Library of Canada Cataloguing in Publication Data

Day, Sonia
    The urban gardener indoors : how to grow things successfully in your house,
    apartment, or condo / Sonia Day

Includes index.
ISBN 1-55263-231-8

1. Indoor gardening. 2. House plants. I. Title.

SB419.D39 2004   635.9'65   C2003-905395-4

THE CANADA COUNCIL | LE CONSEIL DES ARTS
FOR THE ARTS | DU CANADA
SINCE 1957 | DEPUIS 1957

ONTARIO ARTS COUNCIL
CONSEIL DES ARTS DE L'ONTARIO

The publisher gratefully acknowledges the support of the Canada Council for the Arts
and the Ontario Arts Council for its publishing program. We acknowledge the support
of the Government of Ontario through the Ontario Media Development Corporation's
Ontario Book Initiative.

We acknowledge the financial support of the Government of Canada through the Book
Publishing Industry Development Program (BPIDP) for our publishing activities.

Key Porter Books Limited
70 The Esplanade
Toronto, Ontario
Canada M5E 1R2
www.keyporter.com

Text design: Peter Maher
Illustrations: Jock MacRae
Electronic formatting: Heidy Lawrance Associates

Printed and bound in Canada
04 05 06 07 08 09 6 5 4 3 2 1

Contents

Introduction

A bit of greenery. That's what many of us in the city crave. While the urban lifestyle has its advantages, one drawback is that we tend to have no connection with nature, especially during the winter months. A woman I know who lives in a downtown condo loves being close to her office. She walks to work and doesn't own a car. But she often wails that she's tired of technology and of "being surrounded by concrete" all day— and that it would be wonderful to have something green to look at once she gets home.

This book explains how to fulfill that need. It contains down-to-earth ideas on bringing a touch of the great green world indoors—whether you live in a condo or apartment in the sky, or a house on a city street. You'll learn about all kinds of great plants that are easy to grow, and which ones you'd be wise to avoid. There's practical advice on how to keep plants healthy and happy in less than ideal conditions, such as low light and too-dry central heating. For those who get a kick out of gardening, there are step-by-step instructions on growing plants from seeds or cuttings (it's surprisingly simple, if you pick the right ones) and forcing a few spring bulbs. If you don't have much time to spare, there are some suggestions on green things that will perk up the living room, but not take over your life. And for the budget-minded, many chapters contain a money-saving idea or two.

Finally, you'll find plenty of nitty-gritty tips from real people who grow things indoors in the city. These folks have learned, mostly by trial and error, what it takes to have healthy herbs, or huge, leafy houseplants, or spectacular blooms of amaryllis, or flourishing geranium cuttings on the window ledge. A few work in the gardening business. Most, however, are enthusiastic amateurs who have forged a link with nature simply because they love it.

"There's no better way to relieve the stresses of urban living," one of them, Richard Tawton, told me recently. "I derive incredible satisfaction from my houseplants. I wouldn't be without them."

After dipping into these pages, perhaps you will feel the same way.

Houseplants Don't Have To Be a Hassle

Growing things indoors isn't as popular as it used to be. The Victorians loved houseplants. So did most of us during the 1970s. Back then, you saw greenery everywhere—festooning homes, restaurants, and offices. Just about every window had a trailing plant in it, usually supported by a harness made of macramé—and people didn't throw their avocado pits out. Instead, it was trendy to root the pits in water and let them develop into spindly indoor trees. We also planted orange and grapefruit pips, and were filled with pride when these grew too.

Nowadays, however, outdoor gardening is what's fashionable. It seems that only dedicated green thumbs bother with leafy plants indoors (and the fad for weaving string and wool into those ghastly macramé hangers has vanished, thank heavens). "Houseplants? No way," shudders one condo dweller who loves growing all kinds of flowers on her balcony in summertime, but refuses to maintain even a smidgen of something green indoors. She limits herself to a few artificial silk flowers, arranged in a vase on her dining room table—an attitude echoed by many modern gardeners.

What has caused this change of heart? Different tastes in decor are partly responsible (sleek minimalism doesn't lend itself to lots of greenery), but in addition, the criticism often voiced about leafy green houseplants is that they "make a mess everywhere." They take up valuable space in our homes (which are smaller than they used to be), they're a pain in the neck to look after, and they often become infested with bugs and diseases, thanks to central heating. However, what's overlooked by the new breed of houseplant haters is that there can be real therapeutic benefits to having a touch of Mother Nature indoors (see page 134). And they don't have to be a hassle.

Stick to these easy ones

The trick, if you want a bit of green, is to steer clear of the troublemakers and go for specimens that aren't too picky about their surroundings. The following is a list of houseplants for beginners to try. Hardly any of them produce flowers worth a damn, but their foliage can be truly heart-warming on a gray winter's day.

Chinese evergreens

If you admit to being horticulturally challenged, here's one plant that will probably survive your neglect. Chinese evergreens (*Aglaonema*) are often called "starter plants" by the pros because virtually anyone can manage to keep them going. They produce big, beautiful, tropical-looking leaves in shiny green, often with white or yellow stripes, blotches, or spots. (They have no connection with evergreens, such as cedars and spruces, that we see outdoors in North America.)

The biggest draw of Chinese evergreens is that they tolerate low light. So you can put them in a dark corner of a living room and not worry. Their preferred location, however, is in medium light. They'll produce more leaves under those conditions, and you'll also see more of the attractive markings on their leaves. Never place their pots in direct sunshine (it will scorch the foliage). High humidity helps too (see page 100).

The variety that's on sale virtually everywhere is *Aglaonema commutatum*, which has pointy leaves about 8 inches (20 cm) long. Another variety, called *A. crispum* (which has the rather sinister nickname of "painted drop-tongue"), has bigger, leathery leaves in gray-green.

This houseplant is grown mostly for its leaves. But it belongs to a family of plants called aroids—and like its outdoor cousin, Jack in the Pulpit, it will sometimes send up a whitish stalk that unfurls, flag-like, followed by pretty bright red fruit that resembles holly berries. If that happens, congratulations. It's a sign your Chinese evergreen is healthy and happy.

As the plant ages, fat, rough-looking stems will develop, with leaves clustered on top, like a headdress. Eventually, you may get lots of stem and very little foliage. That's when it's time to give your Chinese evergreen the chop and make a new one. Cut the top section of the stem off and re-root it (see page 78).

Croton

Croton's leathery leaves are so colorful the plant has the nickname "Joseph's coat." The leaves come in lurid combinations of yellow and green, red and green, and even yellow and orange. In the tropics, crotons (*Codiaeum variegatum pictum*) are cultivated as big, bushy garden shrubs. They're great indoors because their bold hues will brighten any room—and they act as a nice "anchor" to a grouping of green leafy plants. They need lots of light (but preferably not direct sunshine) and, most important, high humidity. Without the latter, spider mites can completely cripple crotons in the space of a few weeks.

Devil's ivy

A trailing plant seen everywhere, devil's ivy goes under three Latin names nowadays—*Pothos*, *Scindapsus*, or *Epipremnum*. No matter. It's virtually foolproof. The variety sold most often is *S. aureus*, which churns out bright green leaves blotched with yellow or white bits. It tolerates most temperatures, doesn't mind low light, and keeps on growing. If it gets overwhelming, chop the trailing stems off, preferably in spring.

Dieffenbachia

Fussy types won't have this plant around because of its much-vaunted ability to strike dumb any warm-blooded creature that dines on it. (Its nickname is "dumbcane." See page 132.) If you have kitties that nibble everything they can lay their troublesome little paws on, it's probably best to avoid dieffenbachia. But in pet-free households, this is a delightful plant that's easy to grow. It develops fat stems carrying very decorative large leaves, in green mottled with white.

Give dieffenbachia high humidity, warmth, and bright light (but not direct sunshine), and they'll usually thrive, sometimes growing tall. But one drawback as this plant ages is that lower leaves may dry up and fall off. Then you're stuck with an uninspiring stick of a stem carrying only the odd bit of greenery. When that happens, decapitate the plant, cut a center section of stem off, and root it sideways (see page 83).

Be sure to wear gloves, or wash your hands after picking off dead leaves or taking cuttings from dieffenbachia. The poisonous sap can irritate skin.

Dracaena

One variety of dracaena, *D. marginata*, should be called the "office plant." Sad-looking specimens of it sit in corners of corporate offices everywhere—ignored and neglected. It has clusters of spiky, grass-like leaves with sharp edges (so sharp they can actually inflict a cut, as paper sometimes does) bunched on top of wobbly stems that look a bit like snakes. *D. marginata* survives virtually everywhere because it's one of the toughest plants on the planet. It will cling on even if the light is dreadful and you forget to water it for months. However, if treated kindly, this type of dracaena can soar into an attractive-looking tree up to 10 feet (3 m) high. Magnificent specimens of *D. marginata* sometimes grace the glassed-in areas of shopping malls.

There are many other kinds of dracaena too—some difficult, some durable. They all do best in bright, filtered light—but not direct sunshine. Position them behind a thin curtain or blind if you face south or west. When they're churning out leaves, keep the soil mix moist but not waterlogged. Ease back on watering during their winter resting period. Two of the easier varieties are:

🌸 **D. fragrans:** Quite unlike *D. marginata*, this one produces big glossy green leaves that arch attractively out of pots. It's called *D. fragrans* because its flowers are scented—but they seldom appear indoors. The stripy-leafed varieties, such as *D.f.* 'Lindenii' and *D.f.* 'Massangeana' are the most eye-catching. After a few years, these plants will start shedding their lower leaves, so you wind up with a stem, topped by a leafy clump (not to worry, it looks rather chic).

Avoid going overboard when buying houseplants for the first time. It's easy to spend too much on exotic-looking purchases and to come home with too many plants. But don't necessarily buy "small." One big houseplant can really liven up a dull room—and it's a lot cheaper than redecorating or getting a new sofa.

❀ ***D. surculosa* (or *D. godseffiana*):** Commonly called the gold-dust or spotted-leaf dracaena. Its leaves are very striking—big, luscious, and spotted with cream—and in the right conditions, it will produce them profusely.

Goldfish plant

Florists often recommend this cheerful plant to beginners because it doesn't mind being neglected. A native of Costa Rica, and a member of the huge gesneriad family, "Goldie" trails nicely out of pots, producing shiny, dark green leaves and (if you supply enough light and fertilizer) orange flowers that resemble goldfish or red flowers with orange borders. Don't overwater this plant, though (it hates wet feet), and leave it alone (repotting isn't appreciated). Given the right conditions, it will last for years, blooming frequently. Goldfish plant is also sometimes known in horticultural circles by the hideous mouthful of a name *Hypocrita radicans*—or *Nematanthus gregarius*—but most people (fortunately) use its nickname only.

Hibiscus

This is one houseplant that does produce gorgeous flowers. Although the foliage is nothing special, the blooms—in peach, pink, white, and red—are to die for, especially when they appear in the middle of the winter. They usually last only a day before shriveling up.

Although it's a fave houseplant, hibiscus (*Malvaceae*) can actually be quite a handful indoors. Down south, in the Caribbean and Mexico, it grows into a bushy shrub—way too large to fit in most North American living rooms. As a result, growers usually treat the potted specimens we buy with a growth retardant to keep them a manageable size. That's fine. It works. But eventually, the effect of this retardant can wear off—and you may suddenly find branches of your hibiscus exploding in all directions. To stop this happening (the plant will develop an ugly shape if you let it continue), don't be afraid to get the pruners out. Shape your hibiscus every spring—and if you can, put the pot outside for the summer. It loves a taste of fresh air and will often do spectacularly well in a sunny setting. But be sure to bring it in before frost hits.

Indoors, hibiscus is prone to attacks by spider mites. To avoid outbreaks, give it lots of humidity.

Jade plant

Lazy gardeners should jump for joy over the jade plant (*Crassula argentea*). It requires virtually no maintenance and will occupy the same pot for years without complaint. (In fact, it should really be called the "tortoise tree" because of its ability to keep plodding on and on.) You often see monstrous jade plants sitting in windows of Chinese restaurants. Ignored and rarely watered, they just keep on quietly growing bigger, eventually spreading all over the glass. Neglected in this fashion, jade plants wind up looking rather strange. They develop fat trunks and stubby branches, ornamented by only a few sparse leaves clinging to the ends. Both branches and leaves may periodically break off and fall to the floor. (But it's easy to turn them into new plants. See page 82.) However, when it's well cared for, jade plant is remarkably handsome. Its fleshy leaves do somewhat resemble pieces of green jade, and it will branch nicely into a small tree. Keep it in bright light and put it outside for the summer if you can, in a spot that's protected from the wind and not too sunny. It will thank you by sending out lots of fresh new growth.

Norfolk Island pine

Also called Christmas tree plant or Australian pine, this is an "absolutely foolproof" choice for beginners, according to one condo houseplant addict. It produces branches with bright

green needles that darken as the plant ages—and it does indeed look a bit like a Christmas tree.

Outdoors, in tropical and subtropical climates, Norfolk Island pine (*Araucaria heterophylla*) can be a skyscraper, soaring up to 200 feet (60 m) high. Indoors, however, it's another tortoise. Expect only a few inches of growth a year. Even at maturity, it rarely reaches 6 feet (2 m). It prefers medium light, but don't put this pretty little pine too far from the window or its needles will start to drop.

Peace lily

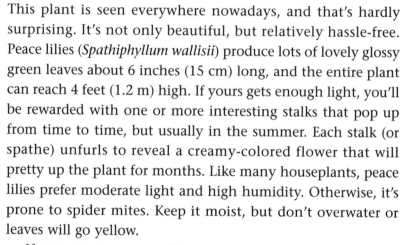

This plant is seen everywhere nowadays, and that's hardly surprising. It's not only beautiful, but relatively hassle-free. Peace lilies (*Spathiphyllum wallisii*) produce lots of lovely glossy green leaves about 6 inches (15 cm) long, and the entire plant can reach 4 feet (1.2 m) high. If yours gets enough light, you'll be rewarded with one or more interesting stalks that pop up from time to time, but usually in the summer. Each stalk (or spathe) unfurls to reveal a creamy-colored flower that will pretty up the plant for months. Like many houseplants, peace lilies prefer moderate light and high humidity. Otherwise, it's prone to spider mites. Keep it moist, but don't overwater or leaves will go yellow.

If you put your peace lily outside in summertime, pick a shady spot, out of direct sunshine (it's very prone to sunburn), and always wait till the weather warms up. You often see frizzled-up spathiphyllums sitting on balconies—the consequence of being hauled outside and exposed to the elements too soon.

Philodendrons

This is a big family of leafy plants that can grow huge (up to 8 feet/2.5 m tall), but thankfully, in the artificial environment of our homes, most are well-behaved. They need bright light (but not direct sunshine) to thrive. If it's too dark, the biggies will droop downward and look lousy. Philodendrons also like it warm—never expose them to temperatures below 60°F (15°C)—and need lots of humidity (see page 100).

There are, amazingly, over 225 varieties of philodendrons. One drawback to the climbing kinds is that, as they develop, they need to grab on to a rough surface. New roots keep appearing above the surface of the soil; in their natural habitat (the tropical jungles of South America), these cling to the bark of trees. Indoors, the best bet is to wrap a flat piece of wood, a few inches wide, with wire netting or sphagnum moss. Then push this plank into the plant's pot. Look for the "sheet" moss used to line hanging baskets. (Don't buy peat moss, which is sold compressed in bags.) Also, try to keep the plank damp. Wet it now and then, or mist it regularly. Don't try to prop a philodendron up with bamboo stakes. They aren't strong enough.

Some varieties to try:

- ❀ *P. bipennifolium:* Commonly known by a host of names (panda plant, fiddle-leaf or horsehead philodendron), this can be a biggie. Don't try it in a small condo or apartment, but it's a great impact plant if you have lots of space. It can rapidly reach a height of 6 feet (2 m), with heart-shaped leaves with pointed tips. Curiously, the leaves change their appearance as the plant ages, and they wind up shaped like violins. A climber, it definitely needs a stake for support.

- ❀ *P. bipinnatifidum:* Don't try this in a small space, either. Its jagged leaves can measure 18 inches (45 cm) across, it keeps spreading, and it may grow to 4 feet (1.2 m) under the right conditions. One advantage of *P. bipinnatifidum*, however, is you don't have to provide anything for it to climb up. Unlike other "phillies," it sends out foliage from a squat, self-supporting trunk. Another variety, *P. selloum*, looks similar, but has smaller leaves.

- ❀ *P. melanochrysum* (also called *P. andreanum*): Nicknamed the "black-gold" philodendron, this one— unlike many of its buddies—grows at a snail's space. It may eventually reach a height of 6 feet (2 m), but you'll probably be collecting your pension before it gets there. Its blackish green leaves with paler green veins are very striking. Shaped like big hearts when young, they lose their curves as the plant gets older. This one needs a stake.

❀ **P. scandens**: A "classic" houseplant that used to be seen everywhere, suspended in those tiresome macramé hangers. It has small, heart-shaped leaves of dark green and either trails or climbs. *P. scandens* soared in popularity because it's one of the easiest plant on the planet to grow. In fact, this one is hard to kill—and it may become too much of a good thing, extending its nosy tentacles everywhere. When that happens, pinch off the long trailing bits or the plant will have a skimpy look.

Ponytail palm

This peculiar plant is fun to have around (people always comment on it), but it's not for neatniks. What fascinates everybody is the base, which swells into a giant "onion," topped by a bunch of untidy, trailing leaves. The drawback is that these leaves inevitably get dried out at the ends, they flop everywhere, and they eventually fall off as the "onion" sends up a stem. You wind up with a squat tree that looks downright weird: a fat trunk, topped by a ponytail of foliage, anchored to the pot by this strange bulbous object sitting on top of the soil. But ponytail palm (*Beaucarnea recurvata*) is a real conversation piece—and it's easy to grow. It prefers bright light (but will tolerate less than ideal conditions), and it won't sulk if you forget to water it (because, like a camel, it stores water in that "onion"). Give it a good soak once in a while and be careful of the leaves. They're so sharp, you can cut yourself on them. Originally from Mexico, ponytail palm is not really a palm tree at all; it's often sold at garden centers under its true name, Nolina.

Prayer plant

So named because its leaves tend to fold up at night (as if in prayer), this is a smallish plant with interesting leaf markings. You'll find many varieties on sale nowadays, but they're all recognizable by the contrasting stripes that run through the center and the veins. Particularly pretty is *Maranta erythoneura*, which combines olive green with bright red stripes and is purple on the underside of the leaf. Don't grow them in strong sunlight (it fades the colors, and leaf edges will go dry), and keep the soil moist. They are fun to watch as it gets dark, when the leaves close.

Rubber plant

If you want something that's really "in," buy this throwback to the 1950s. Like the fridges, stoves, and furniture of that era, retro rubber plants (*Ficus elastica*) are hot again with trendies. And one advantage of this kind of ficus is that it's virtually indestructible. A rubber plant won't usually throw hissy fits (unlike its bratty cousin, *F. benjamina*, see page 25) and drop leaves all over the floor if you neglect it.

Rubber plants have big, shiny, leathery leaves on sturdy central stems—and they are aptly named. Cut a leaf off, and a latex-like sap will leak out. One way to staunch this flow of sap is with a bit of cigarette ash applied to the wound—so they were highly appropriate plants for the 1950s, when everybody smoked. Back then, the only variety of rubber plant available was *F.e.* 'Decora.' It had dark green leaves that emerged from a bright red sheath (that eventually dropped off), and it stood straight and tall, like a soldier. Nowadays, however, you can find interesting alternatives. Look for *F.e.* 'Black Prince,' which has impressive greenish-black leaves and makes a super accent plant. There are also variegated varieties. *F.e.* 'Tricolor' produces decidedly jazzy leaves in a mix of green, pink, and cream. *F.e.* 'Schrijvereana' sports squarish cream and pale green patches.

All rubber plants prefer medium light or a spot where they'll get some sun. However, they will survive remarkably well in low light (the reason they wound up on every coffee table in the sixties) and cope well with central heating.

> **Hot tip**
> "Retro rubber plants are back in fashion. Get one for your coffee table. It's really easy to grow."
> —*Sara Katz, Master Gardener*

Sansevieria

This used to be known by the nickname "mother-in-law's tongue," but in our politically correct times, that's a no-no. Another common name is good luck plant, because in some

parts of the tropics, voodoo is associated with sansevierias. Whatever its title, this plant with the striking, sword-like leaves is virtually indestructible. (In fact, in the Bahamas, it's regarded as a nuisance weed because of its ability to multiply anywhere.) If you forget to water it, sansevieria won't curl up and die. The hard, tough leaves last for years and don't change their size or appearance much, as it's slow-growing. The most common variety is *S. trifasciata* 'Laurentii,' which grows up to 18 inches (45 cm) high and has dark green marbled leaves with golden yellow edges. But there are other kinds, with white edging and gray-green leaves.

Sansevieria look good mixed with rounder, leafier plants such as philodendrons. But for a hip contemporary look, try a trio of sansevieria plants in a row, in identical aluminum containers. And pick a sunny spot. This is one houseplant that doesn't mind a front-and-center location in direct sunlight. Don't overwater it.

Schefflera

This has a charming nickname—"Queensland umbrella tree"—but it's rarely used. Everyone simply calls this leafy plant schefflera. It produces big, tough, shiny leaves that radiate outwards, like spokes in an umbrella. Give it a large container, and it may grow up to 6 feet (2 m) tall. It prefers medium light and is fussy about dust. Sponge the leaves off every couple of weeks if you want your schefflera to do well.

Spider plant

Around for years, poor old spider plant (*Chlorophytum comosum*) gets snubbed as "too boring" by many people nowadays. And that's too bad, because it has several pluses: it's a snap to grow, it produces pretty pointed leaves in creamy white and green that look great poking their way among other big-leafed houseplants, and it's one of the plants NASA says is terrific for removing toxins from the air (see page 134). Also, if you take care of your spider plant, it will keep having babies. It's fun to watch the little white flowers emerge on long stems, then turn into new plantlets arranged in a "skirt" around the momma plant. (These plantlets are very easy to propagate. See page 82.)

One drawback to spider plant is that it grows rapidly and thus gets pot-bound easily. A telltale sign is the leaves turning brown at the tips. If that's happening, tip it out of its pot, tease out the roots, and divide it. Also, although it's high on the hassle-free list, don't put this popular plant in the sun or its foliage will get scorched. It prefers bright indirect light. Spider plant is seldom bothered by bugs.

Swiss cheese plant

The leaves of this delish plant start out looking unremarkable, but later on, they get huge and holey, and are somewhat reminiscent of Swiss cheese. That's how *Monstera deliciosa* got its nickname. Sometimes sold as a split-leaf philodendron (*P. pertusum*), it actually belongs to the aroid family (which includes another popular plant, the schefflera). Whatever its lineage, most people love having this not-so-cheesy novelty around. The cut-out leaves are the main attraction, but in the wild, they're not there for aesthetic reasons. They serve a practical purpose, letting high winds waft through without flattening the whole plant. (On some islands of the Caribbean, where Swiss cheese plants clamber up trunks of massive trees, they're called hurricane plants.)

If you have space for only one biggie, make it an *M. deliciosa*. It's relatively easy to grow but must be kept moist and watered frequently. It does best in medium filtered light. Be warned, though: this eye-catching tropical treat can get huge—over 10 feet (3 m) tall and 6 feet (2 m) wide (although in most cases, it won't get that big indoors). It will need a stake for support. Prune if it gets too pushy.

> **Hot tip**
>
> "Get a Swiss cheese plant. It has real attitude. Everyone who visits my place asks, 'What's *that?*'"
> —*Richard Tawton,*
> *condo houseplant fan*

Tapeworm plant

Don't be put off by the noxious name. This curious plant is fun to have around and will prompt "What's *that?*" comments from your friends. It grows like a tapeworm, sending out a procession of flat, green, segmented stems with no leaves. During its blooming period (usually in winter), little whitish-green flowers appear on the edges of each segment, then red fruits follow. A native of the Solomon Islands, tapeworm plant *(Homalocladium platycladum)* develops into big bushes in California, but indoors, it seldom grows bigger than 3 or 4 feet (1 or 1.2 m). It likes a growing mix that contains plenty of peat moss, and should be kept moist. Fertilize it once a month in the summer months. If tips of segments turn brown—a common problem during winter—it means this not-so-well-known houseplant is begging for more humidity in the air.

Tradescantia

Another houseplant whose popular name (wandering Jew) is now considered politically incorrect. There are many varieties of tradescantias, and they're all trailing plants. Very easy to grow (some would call them indestructible), they look good on their own in hanging baskets or combined in pots with upright plants. They're related to zebrinas, which look very similar. One tradescantia variety, *T. fluminensis* 'Quicksilver,' grows like gangbusters, producing stripy green and white leaves, and is a good bet if you want fast results. You can also find pretty purple varieties. Give them all bright light, with some direct sun if you can—or they'll often lose their pretty leaf coloring. They also like to be well watered. Pinch back the trailing bits if they get too long.

Grow your own coffee

Well, not really. But there is a type of coffee tree that makes a surprisingly good houseplant. If you're patient, it will also cough up enough beans to make at least one cup of caffeine fuel. It's called *Coffea arabica* and, although not well known as an indoor plant, it's very decorative, with big, oval leaves in bright, shiny green. This little tree may reach about 4 feet (1.2 m) high. After at least four years (but often much longer) sweet-scented white flowers will appear, usually in midsummer or early fall. Then comes the surprising part: red "cherries." Open these up, and you'll find a pulpy substance inside, surrounding two seeds that look like peanuts. These are the coffee beans. Let the beans dry off naturally (don't be tempted to push the process by using a microwave), then brush off the papery flakes surrounding them and roast them in a popcorn popper.

To get *C. arabica* to thrive, give it medium light, close to—but not sitting in—a window, and warmth (leaves will drop if the temperature goes below 55°F/13°C). Black or brown leaf tips are a sign that there's not enough humidity. Even if you don't get blessed with coffee beans, this plant is a real conversation piece.

Some houseplants to avoid (unless you're experienced)

English ivy

It's sold everywhere—and gardening books often claim that it's trouble-free. But the truth is, English ivy (*Hedera helix*) can be a huge hassle indoors. The problem isn't growing it—it's bugs. Kept in your average centrally heated, warm room, this kind of ivy often gets inundated by spider mites (see page 120). They can quickly reduce a nicely trailing plant to a shriveled mess—and then the mites will probably move on to your other plants.

If you insist on ivy, keep the humidity high. Mist the leaves every week, and put the entire plant under the kitchen tap (or shower) every month, to dislodge any mite eggs lurking in the soil. And if you keep the plant in a cooler room (it prefers the temperature to be around 50°F/10°C), it's less likely to be bothered by buggy invaders.

> **Hot tip**
> "Don't panic if your tropical houseplants drop a few yellow leaves in the fall. It's normal. So long as their new young leaves are healthy, the plants are probably okay."
> —*Charlie Dobbin, tropical plant expert*

Ficus

The weeping fig tree, or *Ficus benjamina,* is a hugely popular houseplant, with good reason. Indoors, it grows into a graceful tree, over 6 feet (2 m) tall, with lots of bright green shiny leaves that harmonize nicely with any decor, contemporary or classical. However, ficus can be problematic.

One of the mostly commonly asked questions on gardening hotline shows in North America is: "Why did the leaves of my ficus fall off?" The answer is: it depends. Ficus comes from

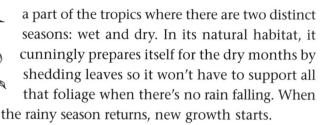

a part of the tropics where there are two distinct seasons: wet and dry. In its natural habitat, it cunningly prepares itself for the dry months by shedding leaves so it won't have to support all that foliage when there's no rain falling. When the rainy season returns, new growth starts.

Indoors, however, leaf-shedding is usually a sign that something in the tree's environment has changed, and—since ficus are creatures of habit—it's become unhappy. Did you move the plant to a different location? Forget to water it? Administer too much fertilizer? Subject it to insufficient light or to temperatures below 60°F (16°C)? Expose it to a sudden draft? These will all cause leaf drop.

If the leaves are also turning yellow, the problem could be overwatering. If they're pale (with tiny yellow spots), spider mites may be the culprit. If there's a sticky substance dripping on the floor, it could be aphids. (See page 121 for solutions to these nasty nuisances.)

Tea plant

Camellia sinensis, the source of the black tea loved around the world, is hot as a houseplant. You will often see potted versions for sale in garden centers. It's certainly attractive (like other camellias, *C. sinensis* produces sweetly scented white flowers and shiny, dark green foliage), but it tends to sulk in central heating. This little shrub prefers a cool location and may be quite happy on a north-facing window ledge. But in the kind of hot, dry air that's prevalent in our homes, it's very prone to attacks by aphids and other insects.

Other plants that are difficult to grow inside include:

- ❀ **Begonias:** Prone to mildew indoors, better outside.
- ❀ **Bougainvillea:** Seldom flowers indoors.
- ❀ **Fittonias:** Finicky about light and humidity.
- ❀ **Fuchsias:** White flies love them.
- ❀ **Gloxinias:** Need indoor lights to do well.
- ❀ **Roses:** Best grown outdoors.

Ideas for houseplant haters

The comedian Jerry Seinfeld once joked that "when house-plants see me coming, they commit suicide." A lot of people feel the same way. They're hopeless at looking after any kind of greenery, and more to the point, they simply don't want the hassle of leafy stuff getting in the way of their busy lives.

If you hate the idea of "conventional" houseplants, but want something green and low maintenance around, try these.

Cat grass

This is usually perennial rye grass or oat grass, and its true domain is the countryside, in farmers' fields. But ever since someone discovered that cooped-up kitties liked nibbling on the thick, raspy blades of these grasses, they've been treated as indoor plants. Cat grass is now sold everywhere from city greengrocers to gift boutiques. The leaves are bright green, and the plants are attractive indoors, even if you don't own a frustrated feline. Try a row of three little aluminum pots of cat grass for a hip, contemporary look. Toss the grass out when it gets straggly. You can also try trimming it with nail scissors.

Forced branches

Coaxing barren-looking branches into bloom is a morale booster in February and March, when winter is getting tedious. It's also easy. Virtually any flowering tree can be forced, but the best bets are early bloomers, such as forsythia, quince, and witch hazel (whose flowers hang in neat little yellow curls), and pussy willows. You can also use flowering fruit trees such as crabapple and cherry.

Wait till buds have formed, then cut branches using sharp pruners (he-man-sized loppers make for a cleaner cut). Look for buds that appear a bit "wrinkly"—the smoother buds are the leaves. For best results, make your cuts on a day when there's a bit of a thaw and the temperature has risen a few degrees. If you don't have a supply of branches in your own garden, you can find them—ready for forcing—at city florists.

Indoors, soften the branch ends by bashing them with a hammer on a durable surface. This will help them absorb water faster. Then immediately plunge them into a vase containing lukewarm water. Big branches look great in any large jug—florists' buckets or recycled sap buckets are all the rage. Daintier branches are best arranged in something smaller.

Top up the water every couple of days, but don't bother to tip it out and change it. If you keep the branches in a cool room, they'll last longer. It can take anywhere from three days to a couple of weeks for the buds to open up—and the suspense is fun. Kids especially love forcing branches indoors.

Lucky bamboo

Mostly imported from Taiwan (where it is considered a good-luck symbol) bamboo has become a hot home decor item. Its chief advantage is that it's hassle-free. You just stick the bamboo stalks in a vase, add some pebbles to prop them up, pour in water (preferably bottled, purified water, the experts say) then watch nice, leafy green growth develop on the sides of the stalks. Add a few drops of fertilizer to the water, and the thick stems will grow taller. (Then you can chop them in half and give pieces to friends as good-luck charms.)

For best effect, display bamboo in an Oriental-style vase. And shop around. Because it's trendy, you may be unlucky enough to get charged far too much for this "lucky" import from the East.

Baby pineapple

Miniature pineapples are becoming the hottest indoor plants on the planet. You can even find them for sale in supermarkets. They make fascinating centerpieces for a dining table—and you can even eat them, although each pineapple won't supply more than a few mouthfuls because they are so tiny. Wait till the fruit is really ripe before cutting it off the stem. The attraction of these "minis" is that they grow very slowly and require little water and virtually nothing else in the way of care. Just enjoy watching the curious way the pineapple gradually gets bigger, on top of its "perch," then toss the plant out when the fruit rots (which will take a few months, under most conditions).

And don't attempt to make a regular kind of pineapple

grow, by cutting off its crown of leaves and standing it in water. This was a fashionable pastime a couple of decades ago (along with rooting avocado pits), but it usually doesn't work. Unless you're willing to keep changing the water, the sawn-off bit of pineapple just rots and turns stinky.

Colorful capsicums

These are sassy little versions of the green and red peppers we buy at the supermarket. Buy them as started plants in the fall or winter, with their fruit already formed. The variety that's sold everywhere is a species of *C. annuum* and is also known as Christmas pepper. The peppers may be white, scarlet, orange, bright yellow, purple or a mix of purple and white. (Try harmonizing them with your decor.) Capsicums like bright light for at least three hours a day, and they don't mind sitting in direct sunshine. The fruit will last anywhere from two to three months, depending upon how warm your room is (they prefer it on the cool side, from 55 to 60°F/13 to 15°C). When the peppers have wrinkled and dropped off, toss the plants out without feeling guilty. Only pros know how to get them to fruit again, so they aren't worth saving.

One perfect orchid

The stark shape of many orchids is ideal for anyone into the minimalist style of home decor. In fact, one perfect orchid (preferably white) sitting on a glass or stainless steel coffee table is a breathtaking sight.

Orchids used to be the private domain of mad collectors. They were expensive, required complex lighting systems, and were extremely difficult to grow. But now you can find orchids for sale everywhere, and some of the newly developed hybrids are said to thrive on neglect. Pick a *Phalaenopsis* variety. Its blooms are gorgeous and will often last for weeks. Orchids require bright, filtered light, a warm room where the temperature doesn't drop below 68°F (20°C), and *lots* of humidity. If you really get into orchids, you'll need to buy a humidifier (see pages 100–101) and some indoor lights (see page 69).

Growing Herbs Indoors

Decorating magazines tout the pleasures of keeping a few fresh herbs on hand to use in cooking. They often feature photographs of well-known favorites—such as basil, chives, and parsley—planted in cute pots and strategically positioned on the window ledges of gleaming kitchens. Accompanying the photos there's usually some purple prose exclaiming how glorious—and easy—it is to grow herbs in this way. "Then you just snip Mother Nature's gifts into salads and soups," the writers gush.

This is an appealing idea, especially when there's lots of snow and a howling gale outside. However, the decorating divas are deluding us. Big time. Growing herbs indoors is not as easy as it sounds, particularly during the winter months in northern climates. That's because most culinary herbs originate in the Mediterranean (or farther south, in Africa and across the ocean in Mexico).They are not like leafy houseplants, which often tolerate poor lighting conditions because they come from tropical jungles, where there's a mix of shade and sun. Herbs are used to growing on open hills, mountainsides, valleys, and coastal areas. They require *lots* of sunshine—and in most houses, condos, and apartments, there simply isn't enough for them to thrive.

How to have healthy herbs

Do
✓ Check which way your windows face. You should have a southern aspect—and be able to position herbs where

they will receive at least six hours of direct sunshine a day. (A western aspect may work, provided there's nothing outside to block the flow of light.)

✓ Use grow lights if you can't provide sufficient natural light (see page 69).

✓ Use a lightweight container growing mix (not garden soil). Mix a scoop of gritty sand into it, if you can (see page 106). Most herbs seem to love a bit of sand.

✓ Trim herbs regularly. Avoid letting their stems get spindly and weak. You can keep whacking herbs back, and they will respond by sending out new growth.

> ## Hot tip
> "Herbs need lots of light. If you have herbs of different heights under indoor lights, raise the smaller ones up on upturned flowerpots or bricks. They should all be the same distance from the lights."
> —*Mary-Fran McQuade, herb expert*

Don't

✗ Overwater herbs. Most of them prefer to be kept on the dry side. Let the top get crusty-looking before you water.

✗ Fertilize. Generally speaking, most herbs don't need to be boosted with plant food—and they do better without it.

✗ Grow several different herbs together in one container. Garden centers often sell these ready-made "herb gardens." While they look nice at the outset, they will wind up looking messy indoors, because the herbs have different growing schedules. It's a particularly bad idea to mix perennials (such as oregano) with annuals (such as marjoram or basil).

Basil can't be beat

The Greek name for basil is *basileus*, meaning "king," and many people consider this herb tops in the flavor department. Basil is also, conveniently, one of the best herbs to grow in pots; planted in the garden, it tends to get attacked by bugs (particularly aphids). Another plus is that, indoors, basil is a snap to start from seed (see page 66). However, if you want quick results, started basil plants are sold everywhere in spring. Replant these in bigger pots. You can also group several basil plants together in one container.

There's a bewildering variety of basils available nowadays—more than thirty-five at last count—and they're fun to experiment with. Some have that traditional "licorice" flavor, others are quite spicy and don't even taste like basil. A few, like East Indian basil (*Ocimum gratissimum*) grow into large-leafed houseplants. Mammoth basil (*O. basilicum*) produces leaves the size of your hand that are surprisingly tasty. The purple varieties, such as *O. basilicum* 'Purple Delight' or 'Purple Ruffles,' are good choices if you want decorative herbs—they look particularly pretty mixed with annuals on a balcony in summertime. If you're a beginner, stick to plain old sweet basil (*O. basilicum*), which is still hard to beat for flavor. If you want to save it and dry it, get the bush type (*O. basilicum minimum*), as its tiny leaves are easy to strip off the stems.

Basil is an annual, so it won't usually last long indoors. Don't be afraid to keep cutting off the leaves and stems; otherwise, it will get too long and leggy. Nip off the flower heads, too (they'll keep trying to form), or the plant will produce few leaves. If you're bringing basil in from outside, carry on snipping until the stem gets woody-looking and tough. That's the time to throw the plant out. It's not worth trying to keep an old basil plant going over the winter. Buy a new one instead.

Caution: basil is highly susceptible to fusarium wilt (a fungus carried in the soil). If your plant suddenly goes droopy and dies, it has contracted this nasty disease. When that happens, throw the plant out immediately, wrapped in a plastic bag. Don't leave it sitting around to contaminate other plants. Throw the soil out, too, and scrub out the pot with bleach and water (see page 104).

Fusarium wilt has become such a huge problem, it's estimated that over half the world's supply of basil seeds has become infected. Look for a new basil variety called 'Green Gate,' which is resistant to fusarium wilt, but unfortunately not yet widely available.

Chives are cheering

Ah, the pleasure of snipping fresh chives into soups! This can actually be accomplished, just as the decorating divas claim, because chives are virtually indestructible, even indoors. The only problem with them is that their roots quickly become too

If you have chives in your garden, here's an easy, cheap way to import the taste indoors during the winter. In the fall, cut an established chive plant back to its nubbins. Then dig it up, hack a section of the roots off, pot this lump up, and bring it in. It will soon send up lots of nice new shoots. Cooks in Germany make a ritual of doing this with their chive plants every fall.

tightly packed in a container. When that happens, the plant stops producing leaves and looks awful.

To avoid messy-looking chive plants, try growing garlic chives (*Allium tuberosum*). These produce flat, wide leaves that are not as prolific as those of regular chives—but just as tasty—and they won't resemble a haystack as they age.

Or look for a variety called Grolau chives (*A. schoenoprasum* 'Grolau'). It was developed in Switzerland especially for pot culture indoors.

Don't parch your parsley

Probably the world's most popular herb, parsley (*Petroselinum crispum*) can work indoors, provided it receives plenty of water. Keep the soil moist. If it's allowed to dry out, those crinkly leaves get bitter-tasting. Although this herb is a biennial (and sometimes a perennial in warmer climates), it's best to buy new started plants every spring. Older plants are tough, will produce less leaves, and have too strong a flavor. If you're bringing a parsley plant in from the garden in fall, snip all the leaves off before you pot it up.

There are two kinds of parsley: curly and plainleaf. The curly kind is seen everywhere and is great for garnishing food. Look for a new variety called 'Afrodite'; its finely curled, moss-like leaves are very decorative.The plainleaf kind (also called flat-leaf or Italian parsley) is preferred by cooks because it's supposed to have more flavor—although that's debatable.

Don't try growing parsley from seed. It is very difficult to germinate.

Moving rosemary is risky

Although it grows wild on islands in Greece, rosemary (*Rosmarinus officinalis*) will cope well indoors, provided it stays in the same spot. In fact, some experts say it's best to keep this particular herb inside year-round and not move it outdoors for the summer. Rosemary is very sensitive to being moved. Horticultural honchos call it an "inefficient high-light plant," which means it doesn't absorb light well and reacts badly to changes in lighting conditions. If you suddenly shift rosemary from a sunny spot outdoors to a window ledge indoors, it will likely throw a hissy fit— even if the window ledge gets lots of sun.

Gardening hotlines are deluged every fall with calls about thriving rosemary bushes that have given up the ghost after being moved inside at the end of summer. Puzzled owners complain that the plant's leaves are shedding (usually from the bottom up), or it's getting mildew, or it's drying up, or "it's doing fine one day, then dead the next." The problem can usually be traced to insufficient light or a sudden change in light.

If you're bringing rosemary indoors, make the adjustment process gradual. Prune it back, early in fall. Then put it in a spot where it gets less sun than in its accustomed position. Move it again, to a shadier spot, a few weeks later. Finally, take it indoors before the frost hits. Obviously it's easier to do this if you stick to growing rosemary in a container rather than planting it in the garden.

If you grow rosemary indoors all year, make sure it gets the sunniest spot you can find—and stays there. Period.

Be savvy with sage

Sage is a so-so plant indoors. The regular variety, garden sage (*Salvia officinalis*), tends to grow too big in containers. Its stems get woody, and once it becomes pot-bound, the plant will stop producing lots of leaves.

Try the dwarf variety, *S. officinalis* 'Dwarf', which was developed for use in rock gardens. It often adapts well to containers. Purple sage (*S. officinalis* 'Purpurea') and tricolor sage (*S. officinalis* 'Tricolor') also work, and both have very decorative leaves.

If you can get your hands on hard-to-find Bergarrten sage (*S. officinalis* 'Bergarrten'), it may be the best bet. Developed in Germany, it produces big, gray-blue silvery leaves. But this one doesn't grow too tall—and it's a very pretty plant.

Grow sweet marjoram from seed

This herb is an annual relative of oregano and has a similar taste. It works better indoors than oregano (see below) and produces nice little leaves that are great for snipping off in the kitchen. It won't become root-bound in a container. However, started marjoram plants can be hard to find, particularly in fall, because oregano habitually hogs the limelight. If you want some marjoram indoors, try starting it from seed in a container (see page 73). Look for a variety called *Origanum majorana* 'Kitchen Wonder,' which was developed especially for pot culture.

Tarragon can be touchy

Some cooks wouldn't be without tarragon because of its highly distinctive taste. (Others hate it, but that's another story.) This herb can do well indoors, but likes to be subjected to a period of cool temperatures. If you want to haul a potted tarragon plant in from outside, wait till *after* the frost has hit. Let the

Aloes are indispensable

No kitchen is complete without an Aloe vera (*Aloe barbadensis*). This well-known succulent, originally from South Africa, is a famous—and very effective—antidote to burns. If you get burned while cooking, slice off a piece of aloe, cut it open lengthwise, and place the jelly-like interior on the burn. It instantly takes the pain away. (Be careful of a yellow juice between the skin and the jelly. See page 130.) There are also several varieties of aloes in the crassula family of fleshy plants. They're all easy to grow in bright light. One kind produces bunches of smallish spiky leaves that keep multiplying in rosettes. Look for the bigger version, which sends up a single stalk and big, pointed leaves with jagged edges that look prickly (but aren't). It's more attractive and won't crowd itself out of a container the way the bunching variety does. If your aloe plant is old enough, it may send up a stalk topped by a dense cluster of blossoms in red, yellow, or white—a nice bonus, especially in winter.

pot freeze a bit on the surface (don't wait till it's frozen solid, however), then cut off the foliage and bring the pot indoors. This will trick the plant into thinking it has gone through winter, and it should start sending out new shoots.

Tarragon can't be started from seed. The only variety worth growing is called French tarragon (*Artemisia dracunculus sativa*), and it's all grown from cuttings. Buy a started plant. Don't even think of buying its Russian relative (*A. dracunculus dracunculoides*) to use in the kitchen. It's coarse-leafed, grows tall, and tastes lousy.

Herbs that can be a hassle indoors

- ❀ **Dill** *(Anethum graveolens):* Produces pretty, lacy foliage, but grows too tall and spindly. Pull the plants out when they reach 6 inches (15 cm) high.
- ❀ **Lovage** *(Levisticum officinale):* A trendy herb. Tastes great in soups and stews, but grows far too big for containers.
- ❀ **Mint** *(Mentha):* There's an amazing variety of mints on the market nowadays. You can find everything from French banana mint (which really does smell of bananas) to Hillary's sweet lemon mint (named after former First Lady Hillary Clinton). The problem with virtually all mints is that they're spreaders, with roots that keep crawling everywhere. Grown in a garden, they have room to expand, but indoors, in containers, they quickly get root-bound and then stop producing leaves. If you want mint, buy a new, small plant—and be prepared to dig it up and divide it when it gets too big for its britches.
- ❀ **Oregano** *(Origanum):* Related to mint. The same drawbacks apply.
- ❀ **Thyme** *(Thymus):* Thyme is a spreader, too, although not as problematic as mint. Indoors, try a pint-sized version of true English thyme, *T. vulgaris* 'Compactus.' It has the same wonderful fragrance and flavor as its garden variety relative. Avoid lemon thyme (*T.* x *citriodorus*). It's a lovely plant that's great to use in cooking, but it spreads

like crazy. In a container indoors, its roots will soon get too cramped.

Novelty herbs to try

❀ **Broadleaf thyme *(Coleus amboinicus):*** Not really a thyme, but a relative of a popular container plant with striking foliage. Produces large, pretty, greenish-gray leaves edged with white. It looks great in a container, and you can eat it. It's treated as thyme in Jamaica.

❀ **Cuban oregano *(Plectranthus sp.):*** Not really an oregano, and not edible. But it makes a pretty houseplant, and if you brush up against it, a pleasant fragrance is released. It produces little fleshy leaves that are rounded, with toothy markings on the edges.

❀ **Eucalyptus *(Eucalyptus globulus):*** Grows into enormous trees in Australia. Eucalyptus deserves to be better known as a houseplant because it's decorative and a wonderful room deodorizer. If you boil some dried eucalyptus leaves in water on the stove, they will get rid of an unpleasant smell quickly. The leaves of lemon eucalyptus (*E. citriodora*) have a nose-tickling fragrance and are the "secret" ingredient in botanical non-DEET insect repellents.

❀ **Mexican oregano *(Lippia graveolens):*** Visit Mexico, and you'll see this sold in bunches as "oregano" in markets. It has a distinctive taste but isn't really oregano. Indoors, it will grow into a pretty little tree, provided it's pruned.

❀ **Vietnamese coriander *(Polygonum odoratum):*** Regular coriander (*C. sativum*) is a hassle to grow because it goes to seed quickly. But this herb, which is related to a common weed that grows in North America, gives the same zip to Mexican and Oriental dishes. It also makes a good potted plant. Snip off a few leaves at a time (its flavor is strong) to use in cooking.

> **Hot tip**
>
> "Try tea tree *(Melaleuca alternifolia)*. It comes from Australia and is easy to grow. I love mine because it looks pretty but is also a powerful antiseptic. If you cut yourself and lay a leaf of tea tree on the wound, it will heal right away."
> —*Sandra Henry, herb expert*

Amaryllis: The World's Best Winter Pick-Me-Up

Some people cope with the long, cold months by jumping on planes to Florida. Others go skiing. If you're disinclined to do either (or you can't afford it), pot up an amaryllis bulb and watch it grow. This tropical flower is the best—and cheapest—antidote to the winter blahs that city folk can buy.

Amaryllis bulbs are sold everywhere nowadays—in supermarkets, big box stores, neighborhood greengrocers, as well as establishments that cater to gardeners. As a result, some people huff that these remarkable plants have become too "ordinary" to bother with. Ignore the hoity horts. It's certainly true that there's no novelty factor to growing amaryllis anymore (unlike back in the 18th century, when the bulbs were highly prized by Empress Josephine, wife of Napoleon Bonaparte, and third U.S. President Thomas Jefferson), but they still have six stupendous points in their favor:

🌸 They are perhaps the easiest flowering plant to grow indoors.
🌸 They produce some of the biggest and most spectacular blooms you'll ever see, and their blooms last longer than those of many other tropical plants.
🌸 Their strappy green leaves look decorative when flowers have finished blooming.
🌸 You can now find dozens of amaryllis varieties, in many shapes, sizes, and colors.
🌸 Amaryllis bulbs will last for years—and with a bit of extra effort, you can coax them into blooming again.
🌸 They are seldom affected by bugs and diseases.

Where do amaryllis come from?

Amaryllis have their origins (like many tropical indoor plants) in South America, and their correct botanical name is the rather weird-sounding *Hippeastrum*. They wound up being called "amaryllis" because of a blooper that began with Linnaeus, the Swedish horticultural honcho who devised a system for naming plants in the 18th century. (Linnaeus made a similar goof with geraniums, which should correctly be called "pelargoniums.") No matter. Few people call these plants by their proper name. You'll see them labeled as "amaryllis" everywhere.

Amaryllis still grow wild in some parts of South America, and if you take a winter holiday in Mexico, you can sometimes spot their glorious, trumpet-shaped blooms flourishing in people's gardens. However, the amaryllis we buy in North America (packed in boxes or simply sold as big, bare bulbs, with labels around their necks and a mess of roots sticking out the bottom) come mostly from Holland. South Africa is also an increasing supplier of amaryllis bulbs. This plant is now so widely known and admired around the world, new varieties are constantly being developed by plant hybridizers in countries as diverse as Australia, Israel, and India.

Commercial growers in the Netherlands cultivate amaryllis in huge heated greenhouses. They plant offsets (baby bulbs that sprout from the sides of a main bulb) from October to March. Then they harvest them by hand—a time-consuming process, with tight deadlines—during the summer months. The bulbs are quickly dried, cured, and sorted, ready to be shipped abroad in time for early fall—the time of year when we northern gardeners snap them up so they can cheer us during the dog days of winter.

Buying amaryllis bulbs

No more boring red blooms

Amaryllis used to come in just one color: red. It was certainly an exciting shade of scarlet, and the trumpet-shaped blooms were as big and loud as a jazz band. But, oh dear, the uniformity. That was one reason many people started to turn up their noses at this plant.

The predictability of amaryllis has been banished by growers in recent years, however. There's now a huge array available in many sizes, shapes, and colors. You can still find enormous, classic red blooms, four to a stalk, if you're so inclined, but there are many other types of blossoms. Some petals have a pointier appearance. Other flowers are double, with such elaborate layers of petals that one stalk is enough to make a bouquet. 'Amputo' resembles a frilly-petaled Easter lily, and *H. papilio*, or butterfly, is as intriguing as an orchid. A few amaryllis make a more modest impact, sending up clusters of small blooms rather than a huge stalk with a dazzling topknot.

Colors have changed for the better too. There are still many shades of red—from crimson to fire engine—but amaryllis now come in brilliant orange, shocking pink, salmon, peach, apricot, white, and striped or blotchy combinations of those colors. Growers are trying hard to produce a purple amaryllis, but so far these specimens, despite names like 'Lilac Wonder,' tend to be on the pinkish side.

Amaryllis is a show-off plant, and size counts. Big bulbs cost more (expect to pay up to $18 apiece for some varieties), but they're worth it. The King Kong types produce whacking great blooms that will take your breath away in the middle of winter.

Monster bulbs are the size of a tennis ball, or larger. Look for them as soon as amaryllis go on sale in September. Aficionados snap up the best picks early.

If you want to get adventurous with amaryllis, investigate the offerings of a bulb specialist. Supermarkets and other mass market stores usually stock only the plain-Jane versions. And check the labels; they should tell you how big to expect the blooms to grow.

Size matters

- "Giant," "Jumbo," and "Superbulb" are big, older bulbs, about 13 to 14 inches (34 to 36 cm) in diameter. They will produce whopper blooms on multiple flower stalks, and will probably have a long blooming period. These are usually the most expensive.
- "Standard" bulbs are smaller, usually 10 to 11 inches (26 to 28 cm) in diameter. Amaryllis sold in gift boxes are usually standards.
- "Miniature" bulbs produce multiple small blooms on several stems. They are charming, and very fashionable, but don't buy them if you want in-your-face blooms.

Appearances can be deceptive

Don't take too much notice of the photos of amaryllis that appear on plant labels and in catalogs. Often, the colors shown aren't anything like the real McCoy. Blooms may look scarlet in the illustration, but may prove to be an entirely different red once the plant flowers. Or the fat pink stripes you anticipated may turn out to be tangerine-colored instead.

This happens because it's notoriously difficult to capture the extraordinary hues of amaryllis in photographs (if you try it, use a very slow film—ISO 100). Also, no two bulbs will produce flowers that are identical. But who cares? Winding up with amaryllis that don't look exactly as expected is all part of the fun.

Some amaryllis varieties to try

- **'Apple Blossom':** A perennial favorite. Grows 15 to 18 inches (38 to 46 cm) tall and has huge, somewhat transparent white flowers, with delicate stripes of pale pink. It's a fast mover, and will strut its stuff within six weeks of planting.

- **'Dancing Queen':** Like the Abba song of the same name, this one's a crowd pleaser. Blooms aren't huge (they usually reach about 6 inches/15 cm) but they sure are sassy. You get masses of double petals striped in orangey-red and white. 'Dancing Queen' is tall, reaching about 24 inches (60 cm), and takes at least six weeks to come into bloom.

- **'Green Goddess':** If you find big, in-your-face red blooms overpowering, try this variety. The flowers are pristine white with lime green in the center, and it's not a "toppler" because stems grow only about 15 inches (38 cm) high, with blooms measuring about 6 inches (15 cm). Be warned, though: the goddess takes her sweet time, and you can wait up to four months for flowers.

- **'Lady Jane':** This showy but not too tarty variety grows 12 to 14 inches (30 to 36 cm) tall. Its big, double flowers in salmon pink, with stripes of vermilion and white, bloom in about eight weeks.

- **'Las Vegas':** A flashy showgirl. Fairly leggy, reaching about 16 inches (40 cm), with shocking pink flowers striped in white. Wonderful in the window on a grim January day. After it blooms, leaves sprout energetically, often extending to 3 feet (1 m). Takes only six weeks to bloom.

- **'Lemon Lime':** This variety produces lots of smallish blooms, no bigger than 5 inches (13 cm), that are pale yellowy-green streaked with brighter green. Grows up to 20 inches (50 cm) tall, and takes up to eight weeks to flower.

- **'Pamela':** Miniature, modest and ladylike, 'Pamela' produces lots of small bright red flowers no more than 5 inches (13 cm) across. Grows about 12 inches (30 cm) tall. Miss Pammy takes up to twelve weeks to make her debut, but she's a charming change from her brasher cousins.

- ***H. papilio*, or butterfly:** This extraordinary amaryllis looks rather like an orchid or, yes, a butterfly. It produces prolific, average-sized flowers, on stems 12 to 14 inches (30 to 36 cm) tall. Petals are striped in reddish-maroon and pale green, turning to vivid lime in the center. It blooms in about eight weeks. Caution: some people find this one difficult to grow.

❀ **'Picotee':** A fave of many gardeners, its name is taken from the French word *picoté*, which means "marked with tiny points." Its heart-stoppingly beautiful white single flowers are large and elegantly contoured and have lime green centers. But what really makes 'Picotee' a knockout is that every petal is rimmed in salmon pink. One of the tallest varieties at 24 inches (60 cm), it takes about seven weeks to bloom.

How to grow amaryllis successfully

Do

✓ Buy big bulbs. Generally speaking, the bigger the bulb, the bigger the flowers.

✓ Examine bulbs carefully before buying. Make sure there aren't any reddish-brown blotches on their sides. (This may indicate disease.)

✓ Open up boxed bulbs quickly. Often there's an anemic-looking flower spike poking up inside—or pushing its way out of the box. *Don't cut this spike off*, even if it's spindly or a bit damaged. Once you plant it, the spike will turn green and recover remarkably quickly.

✓ Lay bulbs in a dish and spread out the roots gently (after cutting off any dried-up bits). Then cover roots (but not the bulbs) with an inch or so of lukewarm water. Leave for a few hours, or overnight. Experienced gardeners do this to "jump-start" the bulbs.

✓ Plant bulbs in clay flowerpots, not light plastic ones. Amaryllis plants can get huge, and you need a heavy pot to hold them. Clay will also wick moisture away from the bulbs, which don't like getting waterlogged. For a change, try rectangular containers rather than the classic circular kind. Square is trendy right now.

✓ Buy a mix that contains peat moss and vermiculite (Pro-Mix works well). If you can add a handful of coarse sand (get it at a builder's yard), your amaryllis will thank you, and will probably last longer, because sand improves drainage.

✓ Put a mound of mix in the bottom of the pot, spread out the roots, and position the bulb on top, trying not to damage the roots.

✓ Tuck more mix firmly in around the bulb and roots with your fingers. Fill to within half an inch (1.2 cm) of the pot's rim.

✓ Make sure the top third of the bulb is poking above the surface of the soil. If it's too low or too high, tip it out of the pot and start again.

✓ Add decorative gravel or moss on top if you want, but it's not strictly necessary.

✓ Give the pot a really good drink with tepid water. Pour the water around the bulb, not onto it.

✓ Put the pot in a brightly lit room that's about 75°F (24°C) in the day and 65°F (18°C) at night. If you can't provide these temperatures, don't worry. Amaryllis are very adaptable. Water occasionally, but don't soak.

✓ Watch—and be amazed—as a big bud noses its way out from the center of the bulb, followed by a long green flower stalk.

✓ When this stem has reached its full height, and the flowers start unfurling, move the pot to a cooler spot out of direct sunshine. The blooms will last longer.

✓ To stop the plant from leaning like the Tower of Pisa, turn it toward the light every day or so.

✓ Water sparingly, but don't fertilize.

Don't

✗ Be disappointed if you can't find big bulbs. Smaller varieties of amaryllis are all the rage now—and virtually every amaryllis bulb, whatever its size, will produce respectable-looking blooms.

✗ Worry if the bulbs' papery skin is peeling off. This is normal and won't affect their ability to grow.

✗ Select any amaryllis bulb that feels soft and squashy. They should be firm.

✗ Buy amaryllis that come in boxes with small plastic pots as part of the package. These pots are invariably too light and flimsy to cope with the weight of burgeoning amaryllis stems. The plants will topple over and become a hassle.

✗ Use big pots. Amaryllis prefer cramped quarters. Hold bulbs upright inside their intended pots before you plant. Check that there's no more than an inch or so of space between the bulb's outer perimeter and the pot sides.

✗ Use shallow pots. The kind of bulb pans used for tulips and narcissus are a no-no. Amaryllis need more room than spring bulbs because they are evergreen tropical plants and develop much longer roots. (Tip an amaryllis out of its pot at the end of the summer and take a peek at its tightly packed roots. They are often amazingly long, twirling round and round the sides of the pot.)

✗ Fertilize during the blooming period.

From bulb to bloom: How long?

Be patient with your amaryllis. They can take up to three months after you've planted them to produce flowers. But most strut their stuff far earlier than that. In the typical house, condo, or apartment, you can expect to see blooms within six to eight weeks. And if they are sitting in a room where the central heating is cranked up, they'll often send up their long green hollow stems, topped by a big bulbous bud, at amazing speed.

Watching amaryllis develop is magical. The stems may grow as much as an inch a day; some people even swear they can see this growth happening. However, a cool room, where the plant can develop at a slower speed, is preferable. Blooms will last longer too. Blooming times—and the length of bloom—vary depending upon the variety of amaryllis you plant and the temperature. Some will have longer growing cycles and blooming periods than others. But once they open, most of the spectacular, trumpet-shaped blooms will last at least a week and often two. They usually bloom sequentially—that is, one bloom will unfurl, then another.

Busty beauties need support

The drawback to those biggie amaryllis bulbs is that they produce such huge flower heads the whole plant can topple over. If this looks imminent, prop stems up with either

- a bamboo stake and a length of raffia, wrapped gently in a figure-eight fashion around the stem; or
- dogwood or corkscrew hazel branches (sold at florists). Pink, crimson, and white amaryllis flowers look particularly delightful offset by dogwood stems, which are purplish-red.

Whatever you use as a stake, pick something unobtrusive that's not going to compete with the flowers, and poke it gently into the pot without scraping scales off the edge of the bulb or disturbing roots.

After amaryllis finish blooming

Some bulbs, particularly the jumbo ones, will send up two—and, on rare occasions, three—flower stalks. Be thankful, not puzzled, when this happens. When all the flowers on these stalks are completely finished, cut the stalks off 2 inches (5 cm) above the top of the bulb.

Long, strappy green leaves should have started pushing up out of the bulb by this time. This foliage sometimes puts in an appearance before flower stalks, but it's usually the other way around. If the greenery grows first, don't fret. If no flower stalk appears at all, however, you've got problems. It means this particular bulb did not build up sufficient energy in its interior to send up a flower stalk (see the following section). If it's a newly bought amaryllis bulb that you just potted up, you have a right to contact the store and ask for your money back.

Let leaves develop all summer. They look as decorative as any other houseplant, and some will grow more than 2 feet (60 cm) long. Put the pots outside in a shady area if you can (but they are also fine kept indoors). Fertilize every couple of weeks with a plant food in a formula like 20-20-20. Try not to let the pots dry out. When they are planted in small pots, they get thirsty remarkably quickly.

Getting bulbs to bloom again

Heated arguments are waged in gardening magazines about the right way to do this. Some experts insist that, like spring bulbs, amaryllis need a period without any light to go dormant before gearing themselves up for the arduous task of sending out flower stalks again. They bring their amaryllis bulbs indoors in fall, stop watering, and let the foliage wither and shrivel in a completely dark, cool spot for up to three months. Then they bring them out into the light, cut off the dried-up leaves, add fresh growing mix on top of the pot, and wait for new blooms.

> **Hot tip**
>
> "A lot of people claim you have to put amaryllis in the dark in the autumn to get it to bloom again. That's absolute nonsense. I just put mine in a cooler part of my house and leave the window open."
>
> —*Veronica Read,*
> *British amaryllis expert*

Other experts pooh-pooh this procedure and argue that it actually damages the plants because amaryllis are tropical and, in their natural habitat, they carry on growing all year round, unlike spring bulbs such as tulips, which originate in the mountains of Asia. (Their roots die off every year, then are replaced by new ones the next.) These experts simply place pots in a cool, north-facing room or basement to "rest," and keep the temperature at about 50°F (10°C). They continue to water (but not fertilize) the plants as usual. After ten to twelve weeks, they bring them out into a warmer location.

The choice is yours. Amaryllis are remarkably tough plants and seem to cope well with whatever we do to them. Some gardeners even advocate doing nothing at all. "Just leave them as is, in pots, carry on watering, and let the leafy growth develop," they suggest. "The plants will bloom again unaided, at unexpected times, like later in the summer."

Well, yes, that *can* happen. However, gardening gurus do seem to agree that a period of "chilling out" (when the plant has an opportunity to take a breather in a cooler location) is required to coax bulbs to produce those spectacular blooms again the following winter. If that's your goal, follow the experts' recommendations.

And if you don't want to be bothered with any of this rigmarole, just throw the plants out in the fall, clean their pots, and buy new bulbs.

Making amaryllis multiply

Some amaryllis bulbs will last and last. Keep treating yours to the three-step formula—bloom; leafy growth, boosted with fertilizer (essential to bring energy back into the bulb); then a cool rest period—and they may carry on flourishing for years in the same pot. Some gardeners report owning amaryllis that are nine years old and still produce beautiful blooms every winter. Eventually, these "mother" bulbs, if they are comfortable in their surroundings, will probably start giving birth.

Small bulblets may develop on their sides, usually after at least three years. Pry these offsets or "daughters" off carefully and pot them up in their own containers. They'll grow into big bulbs in a few more seasons.

Momma bulbs, however, will ultimately become exhausted by the business of reproducing—or just plain tired of living. When they stop sending out blooms and start shrinking (the bulbs will also usually feel soft and squashy, with exterior layers that turn brown and flaky), it's time to pitch them out.

> **Hot tip**
>
> "Try growing amaryllis in water. Use the kind of vase that some people grow hyacinths in. It has a special basin at the top that holds the bulb. Amaryllis grow more slowly in water, but it's fun to watch the roots developing."
> —*Anne Travis, condo gardener*

What ails amaryllis?

Not much, thankfully. One great plus of these plants is that they are seldom attacked by bugs and diseases. Even so, it's important to grow them in an area that's well ventilated and not too hot and dry. In centrally heated homes, they can attract the usual plethora of pesky nuisances such as mealy bugs and fungus gnats (see page 119). But amaryllis are certainly not as prone to these pests as many other houseplants.

One affliction to watch out for, however, is a horror called *Stagonospora curtisii*, commonly known by a host of names: red blotch, fire spot, red leaf spot, or leaf scorch. This disease is, unfortunately, fairly common in amaryllis. If you notice flowers and/or stalks developing red patches, red stripes, or raised cankers, your amaryllis has been infected. Leaves can sometimes look quite attractive with red blotch—they may become outlined in scarlet (with bumpy bits in the red part) or start twisting sideways in bizarre shapes. But there's nothing attractive about this disease. It tends to develop during hot, humid summers when amaryllis sit outside, and it's a killer. Eventually, the bulb will shrivel and give up the ghost.

Throw out affected plants (and their soil) and scrub the containers thoroughly (see page 104). Act quickly once you notice red blotch. If left to its own devices, it will spread and start to disfigure your other amaryllis too. Make sure not to crowd pots too close together.

Buying cut amaryllis flowers from florists

Cut amaryllis flowers are a hot trend. They're pricey (expect to pay up to $25 for each flower stem), but more and more florists are importing cut amaryllis from Dutch, South African, and Israeli growers because they look so fantastic in floral arrangements.

Pick amaryllis stems with buds, not open flowers. Limit your bouquet to one variety: amaryllis in too many different colors and shapes will compete with one another. Buds may look a bit pinched because they are shipped and stored in very cool conditions. To get them to perk up, fill their huge hollow stems with tepid water as soon as you get home. Otherwise, your pricey purchases will wither and fade far too quickly. To do this:

- Cut about an inch (2.5 cm) off the bottom of each stem, on a 45-degree angle, using a sharp knife or florist's scissors.
- Upend the stems and pour water into them, using a watering can with a small spout or a plastic kitchen funnel.
- Plug the stems with a piece of cotton, or put your finger over the ends, then turn them right side up and plunk them into a vase already filled with water.
- Display in a cool location, if possible. Blooms should last a week or more if you take the trouble to do this.

Get Clued In to Clivias

Once you become accustomed to growing user-friendly amaryllis (see page 38), they may start to seem a bit ho-hum. That's when it's time to move on to a new challenge: cultivating clivias. These are bulbous tropical plants that belong to the amaryllis family. But because clivias are stingier with their blooms than their workhorse cousins—and cost much more— they have great snob appeal.

Some folks value clivias as highly as rare orchids. If you tell other gardeners you have a clivia at home, they will probably raise their eyebrows and be instantly impressed. Then, in their next breath, they will ask you, "Has it bloomed?" This question comes up in conversation about clivias because they are definitely the divas of the amaryllis family. Although gardening books often say that clivias are easy to bring into flower, they can be prone to inexplicable sulks. Some may sit in their pots for years and refuse to bloom, while others will send forth flowers with no problem. Nurseries often get calls from anxious owners of non-performing clivias. That's hardly surprising when you consider that an established specimen of this striking plant with stupendous blooms can set you back a hefty $50 (or even a few thousand bucks, if you hanker after a really rare variety).

Is that CLIH-vee-a or CLY-vee-a?

In North America we pronounce "clivia" to rhyme with "trivia," but that's actually wrong. Clivias were discovered in South Africa back in 1823 and named after Lady Charlotte Florentina Clive, Duchess of Northumberland, who was the first person to coax them into bloom in Britain. So it's definitely CLY-vee-a. But no one bothers to use that pronunciation on this side of the Atlantic (and if you do, people will secretly think you're a snotty pseudo-Brit).

Whichever way you say it, clivias have always been highly prized. The Victorians, who were mad for indoor gardening, clamored to get their hands on this curiosity the moment it hit their shores, because the clivia's sophisticated appearance and huge size fit into their glass conservatories so perfectly. However, as with most new fads, only the wealthy were fortunate enough to get clued in to clivias: in the 19th century they were even more expensive than they are today.

Why all the fuss about this undeniably classy but sometimes cantankerous plant? Several reasons:

🏵 They have majestic tropical blooms that appear in huge, bouquet-like clusters on top of typical amaryllis stems. When one of these blooms appears, it's extremely exciting.

🏵 Arranged in stacks from the base of the plant, the novelty braid-like growth of clivia leaves is more attractive than the leaves of regular amaryllis. In fact, it's fascinating to watch new leaves weaving themselves into this braid. The foliage also forms a beautiful, graceful arc over the pot.

🏵 There are only a few varieties of clivia available in the world—and some are extremely rare.

Varieties you may see include:

🏵 *C. miniata:* Sold in some garden centers, this is virtually the only kind available to people who don't have deep pockets. It has gorgeous tangerine blossoms with hints of salmon and vivid orange, and golden yellow stamens.

🏵 *C. miniata* '**Aurea**' (also sometimes called 'Citrina' or 'Flava'): This variety has lemon yellow blossoms that, truthfully, aren't as striking as the tangerine variety. Even so, this is the Cadillac of clivias. Collectors fork over hundreds of dollars for a single specimen because they are so hard to get. Most are grown in Belgium and South Africa. You won't see it for sale in your average garden center.

There's no economical way to acquire a clivia. Buy from a nursery that sells lots of tropical plants, is familiar with their quirks, and gives them the growing conditions they prefer. Pick a specimen that has healthy-looking leaves, not brown or shriveled at the edges. Expect to pay up to $50 for a Clivia miniata *(the only variety likely to be on offer), depending upon the size.*

❀ **C. nobilis:** The original version that the Victorians went nuts over. Not a patch on its cultivated cousins, its blooms are comparatively dull and buff-colored, with green on their tips. But it usually does flower reliably.

How to grow clivias

Buy a ready-planted clivia. (Raising them from seed is strictly for collectors. It takes years.) But transfer it to a bigger clay container because, at maturity, these plants reach 2 to 3 feet (60 to 90 cm) tall. Garden center flowerpots made of cheap plastic are rarely big or heavy enough. Growing mix and fertilizer requirements are the same as for other amaryllis (see pages 43 and 46).

To prepare the plants for winter bloom,

Do
✓ Water very little once fall arrives. Stop fertilizing too.
✓ Keep the pot in a cool spot; a north-facing window ledge, close to the glass, is fine. Ideally, the temperature should dip to 45 to 55°F (7 to 13°C) at night. Clivias cope quite well with low light conditions in such locations and like to have their foliage shaded from harsh sunlight.
✓ In late November, start watering and feeding once every three or four weeks until sets of buds appear. Then stop fertilizing.

Don't

✗ Let leaves shrivel or go brown during the resting phase in early fall. The plant should still look in tiptop shape, unlike other amaryllis, whose foliage can be allowed to dry out before a new flower stalk appears.

✗ Worry about older plants getting too big for their britches. Although they grow huge, clivias like being pot-bound.

✗ Be too disappointed if your clivia fails to bloom. They are very fussy about temperature and humidity. When summer comes, put the pot in a shady spot outside. You might get luckier the following year.

After clivias flower, fruits will form. These take an inordinately long time (usually a year) to ripen. You can grow new plants from the seeds inside these capsules, but it will be at least four years before the new plants gets big enough to produce flowers.

Although they don't mind cramped quarters, clivia clumps will eventually need dividing, but it's a tricky task because the interwoven brittle roots can snap easily. Do it only if you're brave —and very careful. Klutzes may end up ruining the entire plant.

All things considered, clivias are classy, and they're worth adding to your indoor garden if you like the challenge of something different —and difficult. Owning one will certainly engender admiring glances from other gardeners and give you a reputation as a plant connoisseur.

But if you live in a small space, have problems controlling the heat and humidity in your condo, apartment, or house, and don't want disappointments, stick to clivia's downscale relative, the amaryllis. These reward us with blooms that are as every bit as stupendous as those of the huffy clivia—and in the long, dreary winter that's what matters.

> ## Hot tip
> "My clivia often refuses to bloom in the winter. But when I stick the pot outside in summertime—and completely ignore it—the darn plant always blooms. That's clivias for you."
> —Paul Zammit,
> container gardening expert

African Violets: Dainty and Underestimated

African violets have been around for years, and are sometimes dismissed as "old ladyish," probably because we've all seen too many of the boring purple-flowered kinds. But take a close look at these taken-for-granted houseplants—you might be pleasantly surprised. There are dozens of varieties to choose from, in many shapes, sizes, and colors. You can grow African violets that resemble shimmering deep blue jewels, or frilly pink petticoats, or tiny Victorian posies. Some African violets have striking flowers, as big as a pansy. Others are so dainty the whole plant would fit nicely into a teacup. And their rosettes of leaves—which come in various shades of green, gray and white—often look as fetching as the flowers.

African violets originated in Tanganyika (now Tanzania) and were introduced to the west in the 19th century by a German gent called Baron von Saint Paul— hence their botanical name, *Saintpaulia*. These violets (which are distantly related to the garden violets grown in North America) are not difficult to grow, once you know how. Many varieties will produce flowers prolifically, and unlike other houseplants, they don't hog too much space. Even if your condo, apartment, or house is small, you can usually find room to squeeze in an African violet or two. In the middle of a gray January, their delightful little blooms with the characteristic "dot" in the center can be a real morale booster, brightening any room.

Is the light right?

The most common complaint voiced about African violets is that they won't flower. The problem can usually be traced to a single source: not enough light, or the wrong kind of light. African violets that get plunked in locations where it's too dark stop flowering. Their leaves may also become leggy or turn yellow. Indeed, aficionados of this plant consider light so crucial they nurture theirs under fluorescent lights twelve hours a day. Beginners don't need to go that far. Even so, get the light level right and you're halfway there. Other crucial factors are:

❀ watering;
❀ growing mix;
❀ the size of the pot;
❀ the right fertilizer; and
❀ temperature.

Success with Saintpaulias

Do

✓ Use a *small* container. These plants are perfectly suited to urban living because they actually thrive in cramped quarters. Pick pots no more than 4 inches (10 cm) deep and one third the size of the plant's leaf span. For example, if your African violet's leaves spread about 12 inches (30 cm) wide, you'll need to gently push the roots into a pot only 4 inches (10 cm) wide. (Yes, really.)

✓ Park the pot in a spot where it receives bright light (preferably near a window), but no direct sunshine. If the sun does stream in, hang up some sheer curtains to diffuse its rays.

✓ Use only water that is *room temperature*. Don't mix water from the cold and hot taps. Just fill your jug or watering can with cold water and leave it to sit overnight.

✓ Place the African violet on a saucer. Pour water into the saucer, not on top of the leaves. Let it soak in for fifteen minutes. Then tip out any excess water promptly. African violets hate being overwatered or having wet leaves.

> **Hot tip**
>
> "If your African violets produce beautiful leaves but no blooms, gently thump the pot on a table top or squeeze its sides. This will often trigger a 'panic response' and make the violet start setting flowers. Sounds silly, but it's actually good science."
> —*Sandy Morgan*,
> Saintpaulia *expert*

Buy soil mixes especially formulated for African violets. These often cost more than plain potting soil, but it's worth spending the extra bucks because Saintpaulias are very fussy about drainage. They need a loose and airy mix that contains at least 30% vermiculite or perlite. Feel the bag of mix. It should be loose and fluffy, like a pillow.

✓ Keep the plants warm—but don't overdo it. Generally speaking, if you feel comfortable with the temperature, African violets will too. They prefer an environment in the range of 60 to 80°F (15 to 27°C). Like many tropical houseplants, they also take kindly to a constant flow of moisture in the air. A humidifier is worth the investment.

✓ Feed regularly and you'll get more flowers. Mix a water-soluble fertilizer with a formula like 20-20-20 into your watering can. Many African violet addicts recommend doing this every time you water, but at a quarter of the strength indicated on the fertilizer package or bottle.

Don't

✗ Use potting soil. It's too heavy for African violets.

✗ Put these plants in containers more than half the diameter of their roots. They like being pot-bound. African violet addicts say that once the roots collide with the walls of the pot the plants often start flowering like crazy.

✗ Let plants become so dry that leaves wilt. On the other hand, don't overwater. Try to keep the soil evenly moist. Poke your finger in every day to check.

✗ Get water on the leaves. They'll turn brown. Always water from the bottom.

✗ Use soft water. It's too salty.

✗ Allow more than one "crown" to reside in each pot. Crowns are the central bit, where the flower buds appear. If you see new crowns (four new leaves without a bud) developing elsewhere on the plant, give them the chop. Otherwise your African queen may get haughty with the competition and decide to stop producing flowers.

Groom for bloom

We function better when we look good. So do African violets. A regular grooming routine helps the plant (and is a great stress reliever for the plant's owner too). Nip off flower heads as soon as they've finished blooming.

Because the leaves are covered in tiny hairs that may get damaged, don't clean them with a piece of cloth. Use an artist's soft bristle brush or a makeup brush instead. Brush gently to remove dust, dirt, and potting soil that may have accumulated on the leaves. Reserve the brush strictly for this purpose; you don't want to be spreading bacteria to the violet from somewhere else.

African violets can be bothered by the usual bugs and diseases that afflict other houseplants. See page 121 for tips on how to deal with these pests.

See page 121 for tips on how to deal with these pests.

Hot tip
"I confess that I'm forgetful—and I often let my African violets dry out. When that happens, I put each pot in a big bowl, half-filled with lukewarm water, for a few hours. They usually recover."
—Irene Day, African violet lover

Leafing your way to more plants

One of the delights of African violets is that they're easy to propagate. Beg a leaf of a favorite specimen from a friend, bring it home, and start a new plant. To do this successfully,

- With a sharp knife, re-cut the stem diagonally, about an inch (2.5 cm) from the bottom of the front side of the leaf.
- Prop the stem up in a tiny plastic pot (no more than 2 inches/5 cm in diameter). You can also use Styrofoam cups with holes punched in the bottom.
- Mix up equal parts of moistened vermiculite, perlite, and peat moss. Then fill the container carefully, gradually building the mix up around the stem with your fingers.
- Put the container in a Ziploc bag and seal it. Water regularly. Don't let it dry out.
- Be patient. Wait six weeks—or even longer—for new cuttings to "take." Repot as the plant grows bigger.
- Don't keep a cut leaf waiting for its new home. They dry out quickly.

What To Do with Holiday Plants

Most of the plants we bring into our homes become permanent fixtures, prettying up the coffee table or the window ledges or the toilet tank in the bathroom year-round. But a few have developed special significance during certain seasons of the year. We invite these in (or coax them into bloom) for only a few brief weeks—and during that festive time, we want them to look their glorious best. Here are some tips on getting holiday plants to perform perfectly—and on how to recycle them when the festivities are finished.

Making Easter lilies last

We buy millions of them as pot plants just before Easter. And that's fitting. Divinely scented, with pure white, virginal-looking petals, this lily has become commonplace in North America, probably because it's so perfect for the Easter season. But the *Lilium longiflorum* isn't native to this part of the world. Once rare and highly prized, it's originally from Japan, where it still grows wild on the shores of some islands. It came to us via Britain and Bermuda over a century ago.

Most of us keep Easter lilies indoors for a couple of weeks, gracing the living room, then we toss them out when they've finished blooming. However, if you have the space, *L. longiflorum* can be grown in the garden afterwards. Just take it out of the pot, plant it in a sunny location with good soil, and cut the foliage down to the ground. Often it will send up nothing but stems and leaves, but if you're lucky, new lily blooms will appear very late in the summer. Some gardeners who can't bear to throw Easter lilies away wind up planting them every year in their flowerbeds. But this is very hit and miss in northern climates. Some produce gorgeous blooms the following summer; others fail to flower at all. Don't do it unless you have plenty of space.

Some tips for making the most of Easter lilies indoors:

Do

✓ Look for plants with at least eight buds on each stem. Cheap Easter lilies don't have many buds. The bloom count is what matters.

✓ Put your lily in a bright area, but not in direct sunlight.

✓ Keep it moist, but not soggy.

✓ Do the fingertip test to determine if you're watering enough. A surface that feels crusty dry means your lily is thirsty. A wet feeling is a signal that you're overdoing things.

Don't

✗ Leave lilies sitting in water. Place the pot in a saucer, water well, then remove the pot after a couple of minutes.

✗ Try to keep Easter lilies going indoors. Once their blooms are finished, they're uninteresting-looking plants.

Poinsettia pointers

Some people so despise this popular plant, they refer to it as "nothing more than Christmas wrapping paper"—and that's too bad. Poinsettias (*Euphorbia pulcherrima*) are certainly far too prevalent in December, but they're colorful plants with an entertaining history.

The name "poinsettia" sounds vaguely French or Italian but it's neither. This plant is actually named after an autocratic American gent called Joel Poinsett, and it comes from Mexico, where it grows into big straggly shrubs. Poinsett was ambassador to Mexico in 1825, saw the plant growing there, became captivated and brought it back home. Horticultural honchos in the U.S. promptly dubbed it the "poinsettia," but no one really knows why it has become so indelibly associated with Christmas.

Hot tip

"Twenty minutes, max. That's all a poinsettia can take outside when you're carrying it to your car from the supermarket."

—*Andrew Pepetone, poinsettia grower*

Perhaps it was the plant's red leaves, called "bracts." They are what grabbed Poinsett's attention in the first place. This plant is part of the euphorbia family, and like all euphorbias, it produces interesting leaves, but inconspicuous flowers. (On the poinsettia, they're little yellow nubbles, barely noticeable, in the center of the plant.) Nowadays, you can find no less than 150 variations on the original Mexican poinsettia that enchanted Poinsett. Their bracts come in a constellation of colors—cream, all kinds of rosy pinks, peach, pale green, gold, mottled—and they may be plain, or curly-edged, or downright peculiar-looking. One hot new variety, 'Plum Pudding,' is a rather strange shade of purple. However, most of us still plump for a traditional poinsettia— i.e., scarlet—and there's now an amazing variety of such reds to choose from.

Some tips on caring for poinsettias:

Do

✓ Look for plants with healthy bracts that aren't dropping off. (That's a sign they've been exposed to cold.)

✓ Put your poinsettia in bright light, but not direct sunshine.

✓ Keep it away from cold windows, drafts, and heating vents. The ideal room temperature is 55 to 70°F (13 to 21°C).

✓ Pierce a few holes in the bottom of the foil wrapped around the pot. Better still, take this wrap off. It looks tacky, it's not waterproof, and it detracts from the plant.

✓ Put a saucer under the pot and water well every few days with lukewarm water. Drain after twenty minutes.

Don't

✗ Expose plants to cold air when leaving a garden center. They are *very* sensitive and should always be wrapped, preferably in plant sleeves, with more paper wrap on top. If salespeople offer them to you unwrapped, don't buy them.

✗ Give poinsettias teacups of water. They like a good soak.

✗ Place pots on top of VCRs, TVs, or any other heat source.

✗ Pretty up poinsettias with Christmas bows. These plants look best on their own, in plain, dark green pots.

✗ Try to get the red leaves to come back after they start turning green (which will usually happen a few weeks after Christmas). Growers coax poinsettias to parade their glorious colors by subjecting them to black-out curtains and complex temperature schedules—but the procedure is too complicated for most amateur indoor gardeners. It's simpler to buy new plants every Christmas.

A live Christmas tree

If it bothers you that millions of cut trees are thrown out every January, try something environmentally friendly: a Christmas tree planted in a pot. Once the holiday's over, you can put the pot in the garden, or on the balcony.

However, keeping the tree going so you can reuse it the following year does require a bit of effort. First, it's important to choose the right kind of conifer (the collective name given to evergreens). The best kinds are dwarf upright varieties, preferably spruce. White spruce (*Picea glauca*), especially dwarf Alberta spruce (*P. glauca* 'Conica') or blue spruce (*Picea pungens*), are good. The latter come in varieties called 'Hoopsi,' 'Koster,' and 'Moerheim.' Pick a specimen that has a good conical shape and is a minimum of 24 inches (60 cm) tall. Expect to pay a lot for them.

Another option is a Scots pine (*Pinus sylvestris*) or a tough variety from New Hampshire called 'White Mountain' (*Pinus strobus*), which tends to be very expensive. Don't pick the Austrian pine (*Pinus nigra*), as its branches look too open and spindly in pots.

Don't buy cedars, either, as they need too much moisture indoors. Firs are temperamental too, but a dwarf balsam variety like *Abies balsamea* 'Nana' may work. Other options are an upright Japanese yew (*Taxus cuspidata*) or a container-grown holly bush, *Ilex meserveae* 'Blue Princess,' whose red berries look very Christmassy.

These evergreens are usually sold in fiber pots. Whatever you choose, TLC is crucial if you want them to survive. After buying one,

Do

✓ Leave it in a cool spot, in its original fiber pot, for a few days. An unheated garage or a sheltered balcony is good.

✓ Stand it on a big plastic tray indoors and water it daily.

✓ Pick a spot that's as cool as possible, away from heating vents.

✓ Keep the tree indoors for no more than seven to ten days over the holiday.

✓ After Christmas, plant the tree in the garden as soon as possible. If the ground is frozen, or you garden on a balcony, put the tree (still in its fiber pot) inside a larger container, filled with some kind of insulation. Use Styrofoam packing peanuts, leaves, old newspapers, or even pink fiberglass wool, but make sure this stuff completely surrounds the pot. Then put another layer of leaves on top. Water well, whether you've planted the tree in the ground or put the pot inside a larger container.

✓ If you left it in a container, go outside occasionally during the winter and throw a pail of lukewarm water over it. Don't worry if the container is frozen solid (as it's bound to be, in a northern climate). Doing this is a good idea because it helps to prevent the tree from getting completely dried out.

✓ In the spring, take the pot out of its protective container when it starts to thaw. If you can peel back the mulch of leaves and stick your finger about half an inch (1.25 cm) into the soil, it's time.

✓ Trim off any dead bits and fertilize with a water-soluble plant food with a formula like 20-20-20. (Do the same if the tree has been planted in the garden.)

Don't

✗ Bring a potted tree into a warm room right after buying it. It needs to adjust in a cool area for a few days.

✗ Use big Christmas lights on the tree. They generate more heat than miniature ones and may fry its branches.

✗ Leave potted Christmas trees in a windy location over the winter. If you're up high, nestle them close to the side of the building—but if the tree can get covered in snow, so much the better (it's a terrific insulator).

Getting Christmas cactus to bloom

It *can* be bang on the mark. But sometimes this tropical plant with the pretty flowers will strut its stuff in October or November—or it may keep us in suspense until the New Year. Sometimes, for inexplicable reasons, it refuses to flower at all. That's vexing to some people, because the so-called Christmas cactus has become a symbol of the holiday season in the same way that the poinsettia has. Its striking pendulous blooms in flame red or shocking pink are a wonderful sight in the gloomy days of December. However, the timing of these flowers is never a sure thing—and that's hardly surprising, when you consider where Christmas cacti come from.

With a true name of *Schlumbergera buckleyi* (or *bridgesii*), this is a fleshy succulent plant from the tropical forests of South America. Over a century ago, intrepid plant collectors found it growing there in the leaf debris that gathers in the clefts of tree branches. *S. buckleyi* caught on as a houseplant here partly because it's remarkably good-natured about being forced to grow in northern living rooms. But it's also unpredictable. Many gardeners leave Christmas cactus to set its own schedule. "I just let it bloom when it wants," says one laid-back indoor gardener. "If I get flowers at Christmas, that's fine. But other times are fine too."

If you do want to get this plant to light up your living room during the eggnog and turkey festivities, here's a method that usually works:

Do

✓ Starting in October, shut it in a closet at night. You aren't punishing the plant. It actually craves total darkness from 8 p.m. until 8 a.m. for at least six weeks to two months to form buds.

✓ If your closet's too crammed with other stuff, a chilling-out period in the basement (or a cool room) will do instead. But the temperature should be around 50 to 55°F (10 to 13°C). Start this in early November.

✓ When buds begin to form, bring the pot out to a brightly lit area. You'll get more blooms in intense light (but it shouldn't be direct sunshine).

✓ Water when the top feels dry.

✓ After it's finished blooming, prune the plant with a sharp knife or break off sections with your fingers. This will encourage it to branch out. Plant these cuttings and they'll grow easily (see page 81).

✓ Put the plant outdoors in the summer in a shady spot. Never let it fry in direct sun or the branches will actually get sunburned.

Don't

✗ Let your Christmas cactus completely dry out. It's a succulent plant, and needs more water than most cacti. If flower buds drop off, it's not getting enough water.

✗ Expose the plant to drafts or sudden changes in temperature. This can also make flowers fall off.

✗ Keep it in a very hot room. Blooms will last longer where it's cooler.

✗ Fertilize during the blooming period. At other times you can use a regular houseplant food with a formula like 20-20-20, but it's not strictly necessary.

Hot tip

"Potted up sections of Christmas cactus make great gifts for friends in the holiday season. People are always thrilled when I tell them the name of this cactus.

—*Irene Day, condo gardener*

PRETTY TOGETHER: Grouping indoor plants conserves moisture. Urn plant, Aechmea fasciata (left), needs humidity and warmth to flower. The leaves of crotons (center) are colorful, but watch for spider mites!

KITTY CANDY: Cats love nibbling on spider plants (Chlorophytum comosum). Let them—it doesn't really hurt the plant, or the cat.

EYE-CATCHING: A pineapple plant is easy and fun.

COOK'S DELIGHT (above): Chive plants (Allium) tend to get straggly indoors, but they're still great for snipping into soups. Dig up a chunk of chives from the garden in fall and pot it up on a sunny window ledge for the winter.

TINY PERFECT GEMS: It's hard to grow tomatoes indoors. Buy a started plant, with fruit already formed. They'll ripen nicely in a sunny, warm spot. Cherry tomatoes work best, and they look terrific cascading from a container.

COLOR CASCADE
*(above): Amaryllis
'Las Vegas' (top left)
produces spectacular
flowers. So do forced
double tulips 'Angelique'
and (below 'Las Vegas')
amaryllis 'Papilio
Butterfly,' which resem-
bles an orchid. All
amaryllis are a snap to
grow. When flowers
have finished, cut the
long stalk off 2 inches
(5 cm) from the base.*

NOT FOR BEGINNERS:
*The flower heads of
Clivia miniata, a relative
of amaryllis, are a
gorgeous mix of tangerine,
salmon, and orange. But
it's a huffy plant that
often refuses to bloom.*

WORTH TRYING: Not all African violets (Saintpaulia) are that boring purple. This one, 'Chicago Flair,' produces big flowers and unusual, frilly leaves in dark green and white.

PRISTINE BEAUTY: Buy Easter lilies (Lilium longiflorum) with lots of buds. Plant them in the garden afterwards if you have space. They may bloom again in late summer.

SIMPLE SEEDING: Get a plastic seed tray with a see-through lid. It makes starting plants easy. Tip seeds slowly out of packets. A plastic dibber is useful for making holes.

CUTTINGS: Taking cuttings from your existing plants is a cheap way to get more plants. Coleus cuttings are very easy to start in old film canisters.

ALWAYS WEAR GLOVES: Hyacinths (front) are easier to force than tulips (rear) but touching their bulbs can cause a nasty rash.

WINTER GLOW: Nothing beats amaryllis 'Picotee' (left), dainty daffodils, and hyacinth 'Blue Jacket' when there's lots of white stuff outside.

NARCISSUS ARE NIFTY: Narcissus force well indoors, but pick smaller varieties such as 'Jack Snipe.' NETHERLANDS FLOWER BULB INFORMATION CENTRE

PRETTY PAPERWHITES: Easy to grow in water, but beware: their strong fragrance can cause headaches! NETHERLANDS FLOWER BULB INFORMATION CENTRE

HEAVENLY HYACINTHS:
They're the best spring bulbs for beginners to force. This shocking pink variety is called 'Jan Bos,' but they come in many shades of pink, blue, purple, and white. NETHERLANDS FLOWER BULB INFORMATION CENTRE

TIME FOR TULIPS:
Tulips are terrific, but can be difficult to force. Pick varieties with short, sturdy stems, such as 'Pinocchio,' and don't leave them in the dark too long. NETHERLANDS FLOWER BULB INFORMATION CENTRE

EASY DOES IT: Overwatering kills more houseplants than anything else. Check for dryness by touching the top of the soil. If it feels dry, water. If it's damp, don't. A humidifier is helpful too.

BYE-BYE, BUGS: Always give houseplants a bath before bringing them indoors in the fall. Dip the entire pot in a pail of soapy water, then rinse under the tap. This kills critters and their eggs.

✗ Use a potting mix that retains water. Above all, Christmas cacti like good drainage. A good formula is one part plain potting soil, one part sand (see page 106), and one part vermiculite.

Christmas cactus is one of the easiest plants in the world to propagate. Just break off a section and stick it in a pot. For detailed instructions, see page 81.

Try Growing Something from Seed

It's not as difficult as it looks. Many gardeners, even highly experienced ones, shy away from starting plants themselves, for a number of reasons. They presume that it's too difficult, that they won't be able to provide sufficient light, or that it's going to mean buying complicated (and costly) equipment.

None of the above needs to be true. Some seeds germinate and grow into strong, healthy plants with very little assistance from us. You also don't have to spend a lot of money to make it happen. The trick is to try easy seeds first (there are lots) and get simple equipment. Whatever you use, the payback can be incredible. In the middle of winter, when we are stuck indoors, turning tiny seeds into new life seems like a miracle. You will be awestruck. Even old hands at the ritual of seed-starting admit that they still get a rush when they discover a new batch of seedlings popping up.

Some seeds will germinate quickly in warm surroundings. It may take hours, days, or weeks. Other tricky specimens will keep us in suspense for months—or even years. But whatever the incubation period, the end result is usually uplifting and satisfying. It reminds us that, while everything may look dead outside, the spring will eventually return and turn everything green again.

Raising plants from seed also has a practical advantage: it's cheap. With gardening becoming the number one pastime in North America, everything is getting expensive. Why pay huge prices for plants you can grow yourself? Savvy gardeners eventually turn to starting their own plants from seed, simply because it pays. You can grow dozens of plants for less than the price garden centers charge for a single specimen.

The marvel of seeds

Once you get into growing plants from scratch rather than buying ready-planted ones at the garden center, it's easy to become utterly fascinated by their humble beginnings. Look closely at seeds. They come in all shapes, sizes, and colors. Some seeds are the size of a pinhead and a few are even tinier (you can't examine them properly without a magnifying glass). Others resemble grains of rice, or graceful little urns, or throat lozenges. They may be tufty, rock hard, or black and shiny like a patent leather shoe. Several seeds have a positively sinister feel and appearance—the castor bean (*Ricinus communis*) is one—and they can be deadly if used in the wrong way. (Terrorists have turned the active ingredient (ricin) in *Ricinus* into a poison so powerful it could wipe out entire cities if mixed into the water supply.)

Seeds, in short, vary drastically, and so do their growing requirements. Some like it hot; others prefer it on the chilly side. While many will germinate easily, a few may take an astounding amount of time to get going. Try growing a common garden plant, Solomon's seal (*Polygonatum*), from seed and you'll wait up to eighteen months before a seedling pops up in your tray. Never presume that you can treat all seeds in the same way.

If you're a beginner, start the seeds of annual plants first. They are generally easier to cope with than those of perennial plants—and you'll usually see results faster.

And if you don't want to fiddle and fuss, steer clear of two important words beginning with S: "stratification" and "scarification." The former means a period of cold and darkness and is necessary for some stubborn seeds, to kick-start them into germinating. The latter means nicking or chipping seed coats to release the embryo inside. Some armor-plated types must be subjected to this treatment. Plants that have to be started from "fresh seed" are also best avoided by beginners.

Easy seeds to try

Herbs
- ❀ **Annual pot marjoram**
- ❀ **Basil:** Most varieties of basil are a joy to grow from seed.
- ❀ **Dill:** Great, but watch it. Seedlings grow very tall. Pull them out before they hit the grow lights.

Don't bother with:
- ❀ **Rosemary:** Very tricky from seed indoors.
- ❀ **Perennial oregano:** Too slow.
- ❀ **Mint:** Planting a piece of root is preferable.
- ❀ **Parsley:** Seed is extremely slow to germinate.

Flowers and foliage plants
- ❀ Black-eyed Susans (*Rudbeckia*)
- ❀ Coleus
- ❀ Coreopsis
- ❀ Cosmos
- ❀ Flowering tobacco (*Nicotiana sylvestris*)
- ❀ Hollyhocks (*Althaea*)
- ❀ Licorice vine (*Helichrysum petiolare*)
- ❀ Mallow (*Malva*)
- ❀ Pot marigolds (*Calendula*)
- ❀ Snapdragons (*Antirrhinums*)
- ❀ Sunflowers (*Helianthus*)

Seeds need bright light

The most crucial factor in getting plants to grow from seed is light. Lots of it. Most plants need at least fourteen hours of light a day to thrive. That's a tall order for most urban gardeners. There are really only two ways to provide plants with the lighting conditions they crave:

A superbly sunny window
In a house, condo, or apartment that faces south, you may have a spot that fills the bill. But the operative word is "may." Bear in mind that the sun doesn't rise particularly high in the

sky in northern climates during the winter, and it sets much more quickly in the evening. Even if the view from your window is smack south, and you're not shaded by other buildings during the day (a common drawback in densely populated cities), there still may not be enough sunlight for seedlings to grow properly.

Another point to remember: seeds need to be positioned right next to the window, not on a coffee table or bookcase a few feet away from it. That means you'll require a wide window ledge (a rare commodity in most modern condos and houses) on which to stand them.

Seeds started on windowsills also have to be watched constantly. The moment you see them straining sideways, towards the light, it's time to turn their containers so plants will straighten up again.

Many seeds get off to a promising start on windowsills, thrilling their owners. But then their stems get leggy and weak. If yours wind up looking like bits of pale thread and start toppling over, they simply aren't getting enough light.

Artificial lights

People often resist getting artificial lights because they assume they'll be expensive, use a whacking amount of electricity, and be a hassle to install. That certainly is the case with high-intensity grow lighting systems that have metal halide (MH) or high-pressure sodium (HPS) tubes. There is a bewildering array of these systems on the market now, they cost a bundle, and you need to be a rocket scientist to understand the catalogues sent out by the manufacturers.

Don't let the bewildering jargon about "blasters" and "ballasts" put you off, though. The high-tech lighting stuff is designed for pros who want to raise tomatoes from seed indoors, or cosset ultra-finicky things such as rare orchids. The truth is, only a basic lighting system is necessary to grow most plants. A couple of standard fluorescent tubes will do the job nicely. Here's how to set up a satisfactory system:

- Buy a ready-made unit that takes two fluorescent tubes from a hardware store or home renovation center. They don't cost much and come in various lengths.
- Longer tubes are a better bet if you have space. The cost of electrical power for long tubes versus short ones is virtually the same—and you'll soon find that containers of seeds take up a quite a lot of room. Also, light is weaker at the ends of tubes, so for best results your seedlings need to be clustered together under the tubes' midsection.
- Buy one cool tube and one daylight (or warm) tube for the unit. Opinions are divided on the merits of "cool" versus "warm" tubes, but many experienced seed-starters say it's best to have one of each.
- Suspend the unit from the ceiling, using strong hooks and plugs. Attach chains (or ropes) and add pulleys so you can move the lights up and down. Being able to adjust the height of the unit is a plus because, to grow properly, most seedlings should be no more than 4 inches (10 cm) from the light source; you can raise the lights as the plants develop.
- In a small space, attach a fluorescent tube unit to the underside of a shelf. If the shelf beneath the unit is too far from the lights, elevate your seed tray—using a pile of books, perhaps.
- If you're feeling flush, buy a made-for-the-job plant stand equipped with lights, trays, and shelves that slide up and down. These are terrific. They accommodate dozens of plants, but they're pricey. Try starting a few seeds with a basic, inexpensive system first, to see if you enjoy it. And watch ads in horticultural society newsletters if you start hankering after a plant stand. Secondhand ones are often advertised for sale.

Old milk cartons? Nope, a seed tray is simpler

A plastic seed-starting tray with a see-through lid is a boon. These are sold at garden centers and hardware stores in late winter and they're dirt cheap (a few dollars apiece). Trays are usually oblong or square, and they come with a collection of plastic cell paks, which fit neatly inside the tray. Each pak is then divided into little compartments (usually four or six compartments to a pak).

Trays are what many experienced gardeners use. They're terrific because they make seed-starting simple and straightforward. Gardening books often advocate recycling containers— old milk cartons, coffee cans, and so on—and using them will help the environment and make you feel virtuous. But if you're a beginner, say to heck with what's right for once. Go for the "guilt" of a bought plastic tray, because it's much easier.

Containers such as milk cartons are adequate for starting seeds, but they're a hassle. You have to cut the cartons down to a manageable size, wash them thoroughly, punch holes in the bottom, and place plastic wrap on top of the incubating seeds. Then you must keep peeling this wrap back to check if the growing medium is still moist (taking care not to bunch the wrap up lest it stick together in a wad and become unusable). Finding saucers that fit well underneath square containers is also a chore.

> ## Hot tip
> "Plant at least three seeds in every section of a cell pak. One may not germinate. Another may not grow well. But with three, you're safe."
> —*Cathie Cox, seed-starting expert*

By contrast, seed trays are designed for the job. These marvelous inventions catch the drips when you're watering (no more ruined coffee tables). But their most useful aspect is their see-through lids. You can watch your seeds' progress through these lids, then simply lift the lids off to mist the seeds or water seedlings. It's also a snap to start a few seeds—or many different ones—in one tray.

If you feel guilty about buying a plastic tray, remember that you can reuse it next winter. Just wash it out first (see page 104).

Cleanliness helps

When starting seeds, keep everything as squeaky clean as a hospital operating room. The first step in this direction can be summed up in three words: sterile, soil-less mix. A growing medium that's absolutely free of potential nasties in the disease or bug department is a must. Don't be tempted to use up old potting mix you have lying around, or to recycle the stuff your dead dieffenbachia is sitting in. And definitely don't dig up soil from the garden. Instead, go out buy a bag of mix that's specially formulated for the job.

Seed-starting mixes are usually labeled as such at garden centers. They contain mostly peat moss, with some vermiculite or perlite. Sometimes fertilizer is thrown in too. Whatever the contents, they've all been exposed to high temperatures to kill bacteria.

Avoid mixes that contain fertilizers. These can have weird side effects because the additives are often too strong. If they're nitrogen-heavy, your seed tray may develop a distressing green fuzz all over the top. Tender seedlings can also be stunted or completely fried by an overdose of fertilizer.

It's best to add fertilizer yourself, because you can control how much the plants get. An ordinary plant food in a 20-20-20 formula (such as Miracle-Gro) works fine. If you want to go organic, fish emulsion fertilizers do the job well, too. But don't mix fertilizers in your watering jug at the strength indicated on the bottle. This stuff needs to be diluted for seeds—a lot. See page 75.

Other equipment to buy

- ❀ Something to water plants with. If you use a watering can, get one with a long spout, not a wide nozzle (it will make a mess everywhere). A tall plastic jug is good, as it's easy to mix fertilizer into it.
- ❀ A plastic spray bottle for misting plants. There are some very fancy misters on the market now, but a cheap hardware store version works fine.
- ❀ A timer for the lights. Ask a sales clerk to explain how this gizmo works before buying it. (The instructions are often a pain to figure out.)
- ❀ A heavy-duty extension cord that will accommodate several three-prong plugs. The cords on lights and timers are never long enough to reach wall plugs, and you'll need several sockets anyway.
- ❀ A seed-starting spoon. They're made of plastic and cost pennies. Spoons are great for doling out seeds, because

you don't wind up using too many. Get them at garden centers or from mail-order seed suppliers.

❀ A small fan. This will circulate the air around your plants and help prevent the big bugaboo of starting seeds: damping-off disease (see page 77).

Old narrow Venetian blinds, in metal or plastic, make a terrific substitute for plant labels bought from garden centers or mail-order seed companies. Cut these blinds up into pieces about 6 inches (15 cm) long and write the names of seeds on one end, using a 2B lead pencil or permanent marker. (Avoid ball point and felt-tip pens that aren't marked "permanent." The ink will wash off.)

Stick the labels, upright, in your cell paks. Every cell pak in your seed tray should contain a label; otherwise, you'll never remember what you planted there.

How to make seeds grow

Getting seeds to sprout is the easy part. The hard part is deciding which ones will then be nurtured into new plants. Seed-starting requires ruthlessness, because all your new seedlings can't be allowed to survive. Like it or not, you have to systematically weed out the weaker ones. The process of culling sometimes feels like "throwing out all your children," sighs one maternal type, who hates doing it. Most beginners voice similar sentiments. In fact, the biggest mistake that neophyte seed-starters make is to leave too many sprouted seeds in their containers. Crammed together, the seedlings compete for space and light. The end result is that none of them grow properly, and they're more prone to disease.

You'll find it gets easier to play Lord High Executioner the more you start plants from seed. Here are some tips:

Do
✓ Read what's printed on seed packets. Vital information—how deep to plant, germination time, days to bloom or

harvest, special requirements—is usually provided. (Keep reading glasses handy. Often, everything is in infuriatingly tiny type.)

✓ Tear a strip off the bottom of seed packets, not the top. Usually, the names of plants appear at the top. If this torn-off bit gets thrown away, you'll forget what's inside the packet—a nuisance if you want to save some of the seeds to use later on.

✓ Soak your planting mix. Open up the package; if it feels damp, no problem. But if it's dry and flaky, pour a jug of warm water in and let it sit overnight.

✓ Dig out a bit of dry mix before you do this and reserve it in a yogurt container.

✓ Fill plastic cell paks with the damp mix to within a quarter inch (0.6 cm) of the rim.

✓ Tip seeds out of packets *very* cautiously. Tiny ones often come out in a whomp. To prevent this happening, pour seeds into a piece of stiff white paper, folded in half. Then tap this strip so the seeds come out one by one. Or try using a seed spoon.

> ## Hot tip
>
> "Mix tiny seeds with a bit of sand, then put them in a large salt shaker. This allows you to spread the seeds evenly, and it's easy on arthritic hands."
>
> —*Karen York, horticultural therapist*

✓ Push seeds gently into the damp mix with fingers or the end of a pencil.

✓ Leave half an inch (1.25 cm) of space between each seed, if you can. This is easier said than done. Beginners usually wind up with too many seeds packed closely together. If that's your problem, and you're all fingers and thumbs trying to separate them, don't worry. You can pull out unwanted seedlings later on.

✓ Sprinkle the reserved dry mix *thinly* over the seeds (or use a sieve). Generally speaking, you need a layer of mix that's three times the size of the seed itself. Tiny, pinhead-size seeds should be left uncovered.

✓ Mist thoroughly, so the top feels damp.

✓ Put the seed tray lid on and place it in a warm, dark place. (Some seeds require light to germinate, but most will pop up quicker if they're kept in the dark.) A cupboard above a fridge is good. So is a furnace room.

✓ Check the tray every day, without fail. Keep misting if the top looks dry. Seeds must never be deprived of moisture.

✓ Once—hallelujah!—the seeds sprout (some will germinate astonishingly quickly), remove the lid immediately and put the tray under your lighting unit.

✓ Set your timer to deliver fourteen hours of light a day.

✓ Watch for cotyledons. These are little oval leaves—and they're the first ones to appear on all seedlings. After the cotyledons' brief burst of glory, you should start seeing regular leaves develop. That's when to start fertilizing.

✓ Mix fertilizer into your watering container at only a *quarter the strength* that it says on the bottle or package. (Too much will burn seedlings.) This usually works out to about half a teaspoonful (2.5 mL) in a gallon (4.5 L) of water. Let this concoction sit for a few hours, then carefully pour it on to each little compartment of the cell paks. Or water from the bottom by pouring your watering can's contents into the tray. (You'll have to remove one of the cell paks to do this.)

✓ Add this diluted fertilizer into your jug every time you water. But let it sit for a few hours before use.

✓ As seedlings grow, thin out the weakies with your fingers (trying not to uproot the toughies), or even better, snip them off with nail scissors. Be ruthless. You should wind up with only one seedling in each section of the cell pak. It's tempting to leave two or three of these plant babies, especially if they're flourishing. But keep only the best one.

✓ Transplant seedlings that make it to the finish line into bigger pots, 4 inches (10 cm) in diameter, when they're several inches high. Continue giving them mild dollops of fertilizer when you water. (*Note:* Don't bother with this transplanting step if you intend to plant the seedlings outdoors in a garden. Just leave them as they are, in their cell paks. Put the paks in a shady spot outside to acclimatize for a couple of weeks before planting, but keep them well watered. And pay attention to how quickly these seedlings develop. If they start busting out of their cell paks before you can get them into the ground, move them into bigger individual pots, let them grow a bit longer, then transplant into the garden. However, it's a lot less hassle if you can let them stay in their cell paks.)

✓ Store seeds you don't use in a film canister in the refrigerator. Label them with the name and date, but don't keep these leftovers for long. It's easy to squirrel away all kinds of seeds you'll never use.

Don't

✗ Presume all seeds are planted in the same way. Their requirements differ drastically.

✗ Plant different kinds of seeds in one cell pak. Germination times vary widely. Snapdragon seeds, which sprout in a few days, won't take kindly to sitting in a cell pak, in the dark, with other cellmates that take much longer to germinate. Also, plants grow at different rates. Tall seedlings shouldn't be mixed with smaller ones— they'll overpower them. Experienced gardeners put only one plant variety in each cell pak.

✗ Use little pots made of peat moss to start seeds unless you can keep an eagle eye on them. Peat is biodegradable and certainly more environmentally friendly than plastic cell paks, but it tends to dry out at the drop of a hat.

✗ Cover tiny seeds, such as basil, or presoak them. Just press them into the mix.

✗ Slosh a lot of water over newly planted seed trays. This will wash the seeds out of their cell paks.

✗ Forget seed trays that you put in the dark to germinate. If seeds have sprouted into a leggy mess of hair-like threads pushing up under the tray lid, they've been kept in darkness too long.

✗ Position your seed-starting setup close to where you relax, eat meals, or sleep. Seeds respond well to fluorescent tubes, but humans generally don't. This is cold, unfriendly lighting, best reserved for a spare room or basement, rather than a living room or bedroom. Also, some grow light units make a humming noise that can drive you nuts after a while.

Don't be a cheapskate and use old seeds. It's worth buying new ones. A packet usually costs no more than a couple of dollars. Beginners often make the mistake of hauling out seeds that somebody gave them donkey's years ago. Then they wonder why they won't germinate.

Smart folk stroke

Humans respond to a bit of loving. So do plants. Gently brush the palm of your hand back and forth over seedlings every few days, and they'll grow sturdier and stronger. This isn't New Age claptrap. Scientific experiments at an agricultural college in Tonbridge, England, have proven that it pays to stroke plants when they're growing under lights. You'll wind up with bigger, healthier specimens. The technique is called—yikes!— thigmomorphogenesis.

Dratted damping-off disease

Damping-off disease is the number one plant problem to watch out for. You'll know your seedlings have been zapped by this infuriating fungus if their stems suddenly start getting thin at the bottom or turning black. Or the poor tiny plantlet may suddenly collapse. Throw out affected victims immediately. Never give this dratted disease the chance to leapfrog to other seedlings. To prevent damping-off,

- Leave plenty of air space between the cell paks of planted seeds.
- As seedlings grow and get bushy, avoid cramming them too closely together. Start juggling the cell paks around in your seed tray to create gaps between the plantlets.
- Aim a small fan at your seed-starting setup. Position it about 3 feet (1 m) away, and run it constantly to help circulate the air.
- Always use sterile, soil-less mix. Don't add anything to it.

Hot tip

"You can check if old seeds are still viable by wrapping a few of them in some damp paper towel. Put the towel in a warm place, such as the top of a fridge, and keep checking. If these seeds don't sprout in a few days, throw the rest of the batch out."

—Barrie Murdock, seed collector

Cultivate a Cutting Attitude

Buying plants is certainly easy, but it can get expensive. One way to avoid big bills at the garden center is grow a few things from seed. However, it's quicker, and often simpler, to take cuttings from the plants you currently have and nurture those. Watching a tiny offshoot gradually develop into a big new plant gives most indoor gardeners a great sense of accomplishment. Cuttings of favorite plants, potted up and ready to go, also make great gifts for friends.

Propagating from cuttings isn't as difficult as it may appear. As with seed-starting, the trick is to stick to user-friendly plants. If you're a beginner, don't try propagating any plant that needs to be subjected to air layering (a complicated procedure best left to experienced gardeners). Instead, choose plants that can be easily rooted in water or a container of soil-less mix.

How to take cuttings

Do

✓ Wait till there's lots of fresh new growth on the plant. When you're growing plants indoors, this might be any season of the year, but spring is often the best time.

✓ Pick a stem that's shot up quickly and is undamaged. It's probably green (or greenish) and definitely youthful-looking. Generally speaking, don't select hard or wizened stems.

✓ Use a sharp pair of pruners, not some old blunt scissors you have lying around.

✓ Cut the stem cleanly, in one go. Don't saw away at it.

✓ Make sure you cut a long piece of stem—at least 6 inches (15 cm). It should be twice the length of the cutting you want.

✓ Cut right under a leaf or node. The latter is a swelling where a new leaf or offshoot is going to appear or has already started to come out. Examine plant stems carefully and make sure you understand what a node looks like before you start.

✓ Take at least two cuttings of a plant you want to propagate (one may die).

✓ Wrap the cuttings in damp paper towel and put them inside a plastic baggie until you're ready to plant. Plastic sandwich bags with zip-up seals are great for this.

✓ Before potting them up, remove cuttings from the bag with care, one at a time. It's easy to damage them. Lay the cuttings flat on a clean chopping board or table top.

✓ Cut off the bottom section of each cutting below a leaf joint, using a knife (not scissors). Then remove any leaves and the top section of the cutting, so that you wind up with a midsection that's about 4 inches (10 cm) long.

✓ To get the cutting off to a good start, dip the end in a hormone rooting medium. These are sold in little plastic containers at garden centers (as powders or liquids). If the rooting powder won't stick to the stem (and it often doesn't), dip the cutting in water first. (Note: rooting hormone isn't necessary with some really easy plants such as coleus and tradescantia.)

✓ Fill a flowerpot that's at least 4 inches (10 cm) wide with fresh, damp seed-starting mix, not recycled stuff. The mix should contain peat moss and vermiculite or perlite.

✓ Make a hole in the mix with a pencil or a plastic made-for-the-job gadget called a dibber. Slide the cutting into the hole gently. Don't squeeze the cutting.

✓ If you want to plant several cuttings of one plant, use a bigger pot and poke a circle of holes in the mix.

✓ Label the cutting, water it thoroughly, and enclose the whole kit and caboodle in a see-through plastic bag. Put an elastic around the pot to seal the bag. Don't leave it flapping open.

Recycled film canisters are the perfect size for rooting cuttings in water. Use one canister (the kind that holds 35 mm film) per cutting. Just fill the canisters with water and stand the cuttings in them. Change the water every few days. Miniature bottles (airline liquor bottles or food coloring bottles) also work well. But make sure there's no residue left in them. A clean mascara wand is good for poking into bottle necks to clean them.

✓ If you're rooting cuttings in water, use a clean container and lukewarm water. Change the water every few days. When hair-like roots have developed, carefully transfer the cuttings to flowerpots and pot up.

✓ Put flowerpots containing cuttings in a warm, well-lit place. Under an indoor fluorescent unit is best—they need a lot of light to stimulate growth. But a windowsill is fine.

✓ When leaves start to appear, take the bag off.

✓ Wait till a couple of leaves develop. Then start fertilizing with plant food, at a quarter the recommended strength (see page 75).

Don't

✗ Use dirty equipment. Propagation of plants is surgery. You need a clean operating theater, or your patients may fall victim to germs. Make sure scissors, knives, chopping boards, and flowerpots are clean before you start. It's a good idea to sterilize them. Work on a clean, dry surface, not a potting-up table that has soil scattered on it.

✗ Take too many cuttings at once. If you want to propagate from several different plants, it's best to tackle one plant at a time.

✗ Leave cuttings exposed to the air. They may dry out or acquire an infection. Put them in plastic bags as soon as they've been cut. Remove the cuttings one at a time when you're planting them.

- ✗ Mix up cuttings of different plants in the same plastic bag. The rule is one bag per type of plant—and be sure to label the bags.
- ✗ Shove new cuttings roughly into planting holes. They are as delicate as newborn babies.
- ✗ Be disappointed if cuttings fail to "take." Depending upon the plant, propagation can be a chancy business. But you can always try again.

Plants you can propagate easily

- ❀ **African violets (*Saintpaulia*):** See page 57.
- ❀ **Aloes:** Most aloes produce "babies"—that is, little rosettes attached to the base of the momma plant. Simply remove these rosettes and push them into a pot of growing mix. Wait till the babies have started sending out new spiky leaves; otherwise, they are difficult to root. And don't overwater. The top should stay crushy dry.
- ❀ **Christmas cactus (*Schlumbergera buckleyi*):** Easy. Just cut off a section of the stem, including several jointed segments, allow it to dry for a few hours, then push it gently into some growing mix. The piece should be planted just deep enough to support itself. Christmas cactus don't have big root systems, so you can use a small pot.
- ❀ **Coleus (*Solenostemon scutellarioides*):** Easy and fun, because there are many colorful varieties to experiment with. Toward the end of summer, try propagating a coleus that's in a container on your balcony or deck. Simply snip off a healthy section of stem, remove the big leaves, and stand the cutting in water. Pot up when there's a mess of hairy roots twirling around inside the container (it won't take long). Keep baby coleus indoors and watch it develop over the winter. The best site is under lights or on a sunny window ledge. These tropical plants prefer semi-shade outdoors, but they get pale, leggy, and knock-kneed when there's insufficient light inside.

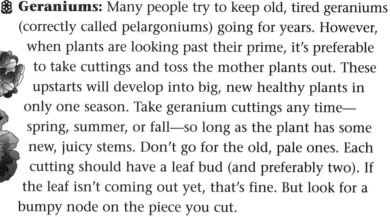

❀ **Geraniums:** Many people try to keep old, tired geraniums (correctly called pelargoniums) going for years. However, when plants are looking past their prime, it's preferable to take cuttings and toss the mother plants out. These upstarts will develop into big, new healthy plants in only one season. Take geranium cuttings any time—spring, summer, or fall—so long as the plant has some new, juicy stems. Don't go for the old, pale ones. Each cutting should have a leaf bud (and preferably two). If the leaf isn't coming out yet, that's fine. But look for a bumpy node on the piece you cut.

❀ **Jade plant (*Crassula argentea*):** Easy as pie. Simply take an individual leaf, or cut off a little stem and stick it in a pot. Side shoots of old jade plants sometimes fall off the main stems all by themselves, especially if you've forgotten to water for a while. Pick up these castoffs and pot them; they'll usually grow. Sand in the planting mix helps.

> **Hot tip**
>
> "Don't keep buying new coleus plants. It's also a wasted effort to grow them from seed. Coleus is the easiest plant in the world to propagate from cuttings."
> —*Janet Brothers,*
> *professional plant propagator*

❀ **Pothos (*Scindapsus* or *Epipremnum*):** These often trail all over the place (perhaps that's why their nickname is "Devil's ivy"). If yours are getting too big for their boots, cut sections off and follow the preceeding instructions. Several cuttings rooted in one pot will develop into a nice bushy plant.

❀ **Spider plant (*Chlorophytum comosum*):** This one's a snap too. Just cut off the baby spider plants that sprout on the plant's long, thin stems. Stand them in water till they develop roots an inch (2.5 cm) long. Then pot.

❀ **Tradescantia:** Another trailer that often becomes too much of a good thing. Cuttings will root easily in water, but don't put the container in direct sunlight. And avoid leaving it too long—these roots rot quickly. Pot up when roots are 1 to 2 inches (2.5 to 5 cm) long.

Dieffenbachias do it sideways

One popular houseplant, the dieffenbachia, tends to lose its looks as it ages. You wind up with a long stem topped by a few half-hearted leaves. When this happens, there's a neat way to make a new plant. First, chop the top right off. Then cut off a 3- to 4-inch (7.5 to 10 cm) section of the remaining stem. It should contain at least one growth bud (a ridgy bit on the side of the stem). Lay this piece of stem *sideways* on top of a pot of moistened growing mix. Roots will go downwards into the mix from the stem and, after a few weeks, you should see a new shoot appear. Just leave this shoot as is, and it will develop into a new dieffenbachia.

Don't throw the old momma plant in the garbage. Repot it in some fresh mix, and the remaining stem will probably sprout some fresh new leaves.

Picky plants to avoid

If you haven't taken cuttings before, stick to the ones above. The following are more difficult to propagate:

- Chinese evergreens (*Aglaonema*)
- Coffee plant (*Coffea arabica*)
- Dracaena
- Most ferns
- Ficus. The familiar *F. benjamina* (weeping fig tree) and *F. elastica* (rubber plant) are best avoided by amateurs. However, two trailing varieties, *F. pumila* and *F. sagittata*, will grow easily from cuttings.
- Norfolk Island pine (*Araucaria heterophylla*)
- Palm trees

Forcing Spring Bulbs Indoors: Tricky but Fun

Smart urban gardeners indulge in a bit of enforcement once autumn arrives. But there's nothing kinky or illegal about it. "Forcing" is the term used to describe the practice of making plants bloom artificially, before their normal flowering period. While the word itself may sound a tad unpleasant (plant "persuading" would surely be better), this kind of gardening is great fun—and the payoff can be terrific in the winter months.

If you dread the prospect of those dreary gray days when there's nothing green growing outside (and who doesn't?), pot up a few spring bulbs in fall and try forcing them. Come January or February, the thrill will be indescribable. It's very satisfying to see gorgeous flowers you planted yourself burst into bloom on a window ledge or dining table. They're guaranteed to make your heart soar.

What's not guaranteed, however, is success. Forcing is a tricky process that doesn't always work—no matter what gardening books may tell you. Some bulbs get huffy when asked to perform before their time. They refuse to sprout. Or they go moldy. Or, darn them, they send up a mess of leggy greenery, but no flowers. Horticulturists force as a matter of course (usually in specially darkened greenhouses kept at exactly the right temperature), but for amateurs this practice can be fraught with disappointments.

The secret is to stick to easy bulbs (forget the finicky ones) and try to duplicate the outdoor growing conditions spring bulbs like. No easy feat, but it can be done.

Let's hear it for hyacinths!

Ah, heavenly hyacinths. If you've never forced bulbs before, try these first. Hyacinths seem to adapt far better to the rigors of forcing than any other spring bulbs. Narcissus and tulips can be touchy, but hyacinths—so good-tempered and dependable—almost always come up trumps. Their frilly plumes of flowers are delightful (especially when you can look at them close-up), and most varieties are fragrant. Mother Nature undoubtedly intended hyacinths to be indoor plants, cheering up northern gardeners in the dog days of winter, for they don't look or smell half as good planted in a spring garden as they do lighting up a living room when there's a mess of slush outside. (In a small room, though, some people find the scent of hyacinths overpowering. Don't plant them if you hate strong fragrances.)

Hyacinths are biggish bulbs that resemble purple-skinned onions. They come in several shades of blue, as well as pinks, purples, and white. A single hyacinth looks striking on its own in a pot. Half a dozen of them potted up together are even better, but bear in mind that they may not all bloom in unison.

Some varieties to try:

❀ **'Blue Jacket':** A fave everywhere because of its classic deep purply-blue flowers and strong fragrance.
❀ **'Carnegie':** White with a fresh perfume. If you like the minimalist look in decor, go for white hyacinths.
❀ **'Hollyhock':** Shocking pink. This striking plant is great for banishing the winter blahs.
❀ **'Splendid Cornelia':** Neat name, unusual-looking hyacinth. Pale violet, mixed with a deeper, purply-blue. Not for traditionalists. The fragrance isn't strong.

There are special glass vases in which you can grow hyacinths with their roots dangling in water. But you'll get better results if you plant them in a pot (see page 89).

Hyacinth itch **hurts!**

Handle hyacinth bulbs with caution. They give some people a rash similar to poison ivy. But don't presume (as many gardeners do) that pesticides sprayed on the bulbs are to blame. Dutch bulb bigwigs say the culprit is actually the hyacinth's outer skin. When this onion-like casing peels off or tears, it breaks down into minute, needle-shaped crystals of calcium oxylate. These get into our pores, making us feel itchy. So we scratch, push the crystals deeper in, and wind up with a painful pink rash.

"Hyacinth itch is not a new problem," says a report from the Dutch Bulb Research Centre in Lisse, Holland. "It has been with us ever since the bulbs were traded." The report adds that the itch "has never been found to be detrimental to a person's health." Even so, it's a good idea to wear rubber gloves when planting hyacinths. And when picking them out of cardboard boxes at garden centers, handle the bulbs as little as possible.

Narcissus: Nitpicker about light

Commonly called daffodils, many narcissus varieties don't force well because they require very bright conditions to bloom. After being brought out of the dark, they often sulk, as lighting is too muted in our homes, even on sunny windowsills. Miniature or dwarf varieties are the best bet. Try:

❀ **'Erlicheer':** A double variety that needs only four weeks of darkness. Has ivory-and-gold blooms and grows about 12 inches (30 cm) high.

❀ **'Jack Snipe':** Has white petals with a yellow cup. Grows about 12 inches (30 cm) high.

❀ **'Jetfire':** A dwarf variety that combines yellow petals with orange cups. Somewhat fragrant. Grows 8 inches (20 cm) tall. Often sold as a potted bulb in winter-time because it produces lots of blooms.

❀ **'Tête à Tête':** A cute little "traditional" daffodil in cheery yellow. Also seen a lot in florist shops. Grows 8 inches (20 cm) tall.

❀ **Paperwhites:** Unlike their narcissistic cousins, these don't need a period of darkness at all. Just place the bulbs in a shallow bowl containing water and pea gravel (which you can get a garden center or tropical fish store). Add a bit of charcoal to stop the water from getting smelly, and watch the bulbs grow. They often get too tall and flop about, but their dainty white flowers are delightful. The drawback of paperwhites is that some people positively hate their fragrance (and some sensitive souls are allergic to it). In a small room, this scent can be overpowering, particularly when the flowers reach maturity.

Tulips: Terrific, but temperamental

Some bulb experts say that, to force tulips, it's best to stick to early-blooming varieties that have short, sturdy stems. But other experts say that's hogwash. "Tulips are picky about conditions," says one. "But if you get the temperature and the cooling period right, you can force all kinds of tulips. Doesn't matter how early or late they bloom."

Experts in Holland also offer this tip: if forced tulips get too leggy, you have kept them in the dark too long. If they're too short, their chilling-out period wasn't long enough.

Some hybrid tulip varieties that seem to adapt well to forcing are:

❀ **'Abba':** These tulips have several great things going for them: they have double petals in a wonderful tomato red, they're fragrant, and they may produce blooms earlier than some other varieties. They grow about 12 inches (30 cm) tall. Unfortunately, they are very hard to find.

❀ **'Angelique':** This unusual double tulip has layers of frilly double blooms in pink and white that look like petticoats. Very feminine. Ideal in pots indoors, rather than growing in the garden, because you can see the layered petals up close. Smells faintly of roses (which is heaven indoors in the wintertime). Tends to get leggy and sprawl. Grows at least 14 inches (35 cm) high.

✿ **'Apricot Beauty':** You'll wait ages for shoots to pop up, but it's worth the suspense. Tangerine-colored blooms are streaked with pink—and it's another of the few fragrant tulips. Grows about 14 inches (35 cm) high.

✿ **'Christmas Marvel':** Pot this one up in early October, and it may bloom in time for the big holiday. Pretty cherry pink blooms. About 14 inches (35 cm) high.

✿ **'Flair':** Buttercup yellow, with red "feathers" on the petals. Grows 14 inches (35 cm) high.

✿ **'Monsella':** A fragrant early double with canary yellow blooms feathered in red. Grows about 12 inches (30 cm) high.

✿ **'Monte Carlo':** Another fragrant double tulip that some bulb fanciers say is easy to force. The blooms are a bright yellow. Great on a window ledge when everything's covered in snow outside. Grows about 12 inches (30 cm) tall and may bloom early.

Species tulips to force

These are the closest cousins to the original tulips found growing in the wild. Some forcing enthusiasts have better luck forcing them than the hybrid varieties. Try:

> ## Hot tip
> "Forced bulbs can be unpredictable. They often produce flowers much quicker, or slower, than the experts say. I've had tulips that are supposedly late-flowering sprout and send up buds in only a few weeks! The temperature at which they are stored is certainly a factor. The colder it is, the slower they'll start to sprout."
> —*Stewart Hamilton, forced bulb fancier*

✿ **Any *greigii* variety:** Very different-looking tulips, these are popping up more and more in flower shops nowadays—either potted or as cut flowers. They are real "toughies" in the tulip world, with leaves that are surprisingly large and wide, and mottled or striped in rust red. This leaf patterning is controversial. People either love it or hate it. Varieties include 'Red Riding Hood,' whose flowers are a brilliant scarlet; 'Yellow Dawn,' which is rose pink with a wide yellow band; popular 'Cape Cod,' which is apricot edged with yellow; and 'Toronto,' which is red with pointy petals.

❀ **'White Emperor':** a *fosteriana* class of tulip, with thick tough stems and big squarish blooms. Very striking.

A forcing formula that works

Do

✓ Buy big bulbs. Generally speaking, the bigger the bulb, the bigger the flowers. (You'll also get more of them.)

✓ Examine bulb labels carefully. Some helpful growers now indicate when their offerings are "suitable for forcing."

✓ If you can't plant right away, store bulbs in the refrigerator or a cool room.

✓ Use any kind of pot—plastic, clay, or glazed pottery—so long as it has a drainage hole. Shallow pots tend to show off spring bulbs better.

✓ Buy potting soil or a mix that contains compost and peat moss. If you can, add a bit of coarse builder's sand. (Bulbs love it.)

✓ Plant bulbs so that they are close together, but not touching. They don't mind being crammed together in one container. They also look better in a mass.

✓ Make sure bulbs are securely positioned in the mix, with only their snouts sticking out of the soil. Potted bulbs are inclined to heave up as they grow. If you haven't surrounded them with enough soil, they may wind up sitting too high in the pot—and they will topple over when leaves and stems develop.

✓ Take a good, hard look at tulip bulbs before planting them. Make sure they are planted with their *flat* side facing outwards. Tulips throw out their first and biggest leaves on that side, and if those leaves face into the container, they'll crowd (and mask) the blooms.

✓ Water well, then put the pot in a cool place *in complete darkness* (see page 91).

✓ Leave the pots alone for ten to twelve weeks. Check periodically. If the tops look dry, give them a bit of water.

✓ Little shoots (they'll be white or yellowish) will eventually appear. Wait till they're about an inch (2.5 cm) tall, then bring them out into a room with subdued lighting.

✓ After a week or two, when the tops have turned green, move again to a well-lit spot. (If it gets direct sun, that's fine.) Blooms should follow in a few more weeks.

✓ Keep all spring bulbs in a cool room if you can. The flowers will last longer, and leaves and stems won't get as leggy.

✓ Prop blooms up with dogwood or corkscrew hazel stems if they get too leggy.

Don't

✗ Buy spring bulbs packaged in sealed plastic bags. The bulbs may be moldy. The bags should have holes punched in their sides.

✗ Leave bulbs sitting around for weeks in a warm room before you plant them.

✗ Add bulb fertilizer to the pot. It's not necessary.

✗ Worry if a bit of mold develops on top of the soil during the chilling-out period. It is harmless, and you can easily brush it off once you bring the bulbs into the light.

✗ Shut potted bulbs up in a closet without any ventilation if you want to prevent mold from growing on the surface.

✗ Fertilize forced bulbs when they're blooming. All they require is the occasional bit of plain water.

✗ Plant forced bulbs in the garden after their burst of glory is over. Experts say they will bloom again, but they often don't—and why devote space to iffy plants that are going to take up tons of space? Your best bet is to buy new bulbs for the garden the following fall. In the meantime, dump their forced fellows on the compost heap.

> ## Hot tip
> "Winter heat in homes is too dry and warm for many flowers. If you mist forced bulbs several times a week, or use a humidifier, you can extend their blooming period."
> —Becky Heath, bulb expert

Cool it, man

If forced bulbs could talk, that's what they'd probably tell us. To bloom, spring bulbs must be subjected to a period of cold—and preferably complete darkness—beforehand. Finding a suitable site, particularly if you live in a condo or apartment, can be tricky. In fact, for amateur gardeners, it's the most difficult aspect of forcing. The temperature should be between 41 and 50°F (5 and 10°C), but it mustn't freeze. You also can't place the bulbs' containers in a spot that's exposed to bright daylight—or where somebody will keep turning a light on. So where? Here are some suggestions:

- a dark corner on an unheated porch;
- a garage attached to a house (where the temperature is unlikely to drop below freezing);
- an underground garage in a condo (if there's a lot of artificial light in the garage, place a cardboard box, with holes punched in it for ventilation, over the pots); or
- a pit dug in the garden with straw or leaves on top, weighted down with a board.

Skip forcing these

Some bulbs hate being pushed to perform before their time. The troublesome ones may produce leaves but no flowers, or their buds may fail to open and fall off, or their blooms may be few and far between, or their stems may get too tall and flop over. Experts at the Netherlands Flower Bulb Information Center recommend that you don't bother to try forcing these:

- **Narcissi:** 'Little Beauty'; 'Little Gem'; 'Small Talk'; *N. canaliculatus*; *N. bulbocodium*; 'Golden Bells.'
- **Tulips:** 'Happy Family'; 'Purple Prince'; 'Mickey Mouse.'

Too busy to force your own bulbs?

Ready-potted spring bulbs are now sold everywhere—in supermarkets, city greengrocers, florists, and convenience stores. In fact, you can find a surprising variety, particularly of tulips and narcissus. If you go for these (and they are certainly cheap),

🏵 Check that plants have healthy-looking buds, not yet fully open. If flowers are already in bloom, they may look glorious, but they won't last long. Don't buy plants that have lots of foliage but no buds visible.

🏵 Skip crocus and snowdrops. Their blooming period is so short they aren't worth hauling home.

🏵 As soon as you get home, remove the plant sleeve (a funnel made of paper or see-through plastic wrapped around plants to protect them). It stops air from circulating around plants.

🏵 Take off any foil wrap around the pot too. It looks tacky, detracts from the flowers, and contrary to popular opinion, won't stop water from dripping onto the tabletop.

It's worth buying pricier bulbs. Order them by mail from a bulb specialist or visit an established garden center. At the latter, choose the ones sold in open cardboard boxes (they're usually nestled in wood shavings, and you simply pick out what you want) rather than prepackaged net bags. Bagged bulbs are cheaper, but can end up costing more in the long run as moldy, broken, or otherwise unusable specimens are sometimes mixed in with the good bulbs.

If the papery skin has come off the bulbs, don't worry. That won't affect their ability to grow. In fact, it sometimes enhances it. But don't buy bulbs that are squashy, dried up, wrinkled, or split. A bulb that's broken in half or missing a chunk of its fleshy layers won't grow and isn't worth planting.

Watch for bargains late in the season. Garden centers often sell off the last of their stock at half-price before Christmas. But make sure you can see what you're getting. Avoid boxed bulbs.

❀ Stand pots on a saucer and give them a good drink if they look dried out. But after that, water sparingly. Bulbs don't need much sustenance during their blooming period. And don't mix fertilizer into the water.

❀ Display in groups if you've bought several pots. Spring bulbs look nice mixed together.

❀ If flower stems start flopping everywhere, prop them up with branches (see page 89). Potted forced bulbs sold at florists and garden centers are particularly prone to flop because they've been goosed with lots of fertilizer.

The Importance of Light

We often ignore one of the most crucial aspects of getting greenery to grow well indoors: light. All of us are guilty of spotting an appealing plant on sale, buying it on impulse, and then plunking it anywhere we can find space in the living room. Then, when our new purchase promptly bites the dust, we get mad. But usually the plant isn't to blame (nor is the store where we so rashly bought it). The problem is probably light. Indoors, the amount of light plants receive—and what kind of light—is far more crucial than outside in a garden. In fact, it's worth spending a few minutes to figure out exactly how much light you have inside your house, apartment, or condo before buying anything.

Check these factors

- which way the windows face;
- how big the windows are;
- the obstructions that block the light coming in; and
- how far north you live.

If your room faces south, and it isn't shadowed by trees or other buildings, in most locations you can expect to receive at least several hours of sunlight a day (that is, when the sun shines!). Facing east or west, you'll get a lot less sunshine. Bear in mind that afternoon sun (western exposure) is much stronger and hotter than morning sun (eastern exposure). If you face north, your room may not get any direct sunshine at all, although that also depends upon your location. In northern latitudes, the sun swings surprisingly far north in summertime and a north-facing window can pick up direct sunlight in the mornings or afternoons, particularly between June and September.

Five types of light

The type of light indoor plants require is generally divided into five basic categories:

✿ **Direct sun:** South-facing windows with unobstructed sunshine for much of the day. If a plant carries a label that says "requires sun" or "sun-loving," it needs this kind of location. Bear in mind that many indoor houseplants hate this kind of light. Sun beaming through the glass can fry them, particularly in the summer.

✿ **Bright filtered light:** Also direct sun, but filtered through blinds or thin curtains. Many houseplants adapt well to this kind of light.

❀ Bright indirect light: An area of the room that receives lots of light, but isn't hit directly by the sun. This works well for many houseplants.

❀ Medium light: A north-facing window, where no sun streams in, usually has this kind of light. So do the shaded areas of sunny rooms. Some houseplants do fine in this environment.

❀ Low light: Corners of rooms that are a long way from a light source fall into this category. Only a few toughies can tolerate this kind of lighting.

Ways to lighten things up

Do

✓ Paint walls white or a pale color.

✓ Position plants against a pale background or in a spot where they can pick up light that's bounced off another surface.

✓ Plant everything in white pots. (This will also create a feeling of unity in a small space.)

✓ Buy some indoor lights. They don't have to be expensive or complicated (see page 69).

✓ Turn plants when you see them straining towards the light. If a plant keeps doing this, it needs a brighter location.

Don't

✗ Leave reading lamps or overhead lights on, hoping they'll help houseplants grow. The amount of light spread from such sources is minimal.

✗ Shift plants abruptly from a brightly lit area to a dim one— or vice versa. Move them gradually, increasing their exposure to the new light source over a period of two weeks.

✗ Presume you can't grow anything. A few plants adapt amazingly well to low light conditions.

✗ Turn a plant with a bud-ready bloom into direct sunshine. The sudden change may prompt the bud to fall off.

Hot tip

"Don't put houseplants too close to indoor grow lights or they'll get crisped. Six inches (15 cm) is a good distance."
—*Mary Fran McQuade, urban gardener*

Get Hip to the Two H's

To cultivate anything successfully indoors, pay attention to two important factors: heat and humidity. You must be able to provide the right temperature for your plants, but what's equally important, and often overlooked, is the amount of moisture in the air.

Unfortunately, in modern homes, it can be difficult to fulfill both these requirements. The problem is central heating. This kind of heat maintains a steady temperature twenty-four hours a day—and it is usually very dry. That's tolerable for people, but not for plants. Many so-called houseplants grow naturally in the tropical rainforests and coastal areas of Africa, Asia, and South America. In such locations, the sun bakes down during the day, but the temperature often dips sharply at night—and it's very humid. Obviously, it's hard to duplicate that kind of environment in the average North American condo, apartment, or house.

First, the heat ...

Do

✓ Take the trouble to check what temperature houseplants prefer when buying them. This information is usually marked on their labels. Most plants can cope with an environment that's 5°F (3°C) warmer or cooler than their desired range. But if the temperature in your home is consistently higher or lower than what's indicated on the label, the plant probably won't last long.

✓ Go for plants that prefer a range of 65 to 75°F (18 to 24°C). They are the easiest choices for most North American homes.

✓ Turn down the heat at night if you can. Most houseplants like a dip of between 5 and 10°F (3 to 6°C). But don't overdo it. Fluctuations of more than 20°F (12°C) over a twenty-four-hour period are not a good idea.

✓ Stick to really easy houseplants if you live in a condo or apartment where it's not possible to adjust the thermostat at night (see page 13).

✓ Be careful about placing plants on shelves over radiators or heating vents. It's usually too hot and dry.

Don't

✗ Buy indoor flowering plants such as cyclamens if your place is very warm during the winter. Most flowering houseplants prefer it cool. Blooms won't last long if the central heating is cranked up.

✗ Put plants in drafty locations. Check if there's a draft by putting a lighted candle in a saucer and watching the flame. If it blows sideways (or worse, gets extinguished), that's definitely not a good spot! You often get drafts from front and back entrances or doors leading out to balconies or patios.

✗ Place anything near a refrigerator. Plants don't take kindly to the blasts of cold air that come out when you open the door.

Watch for the "drape droops"

This happens when plants are shut between a heavy curtain and a window on a cold night—and it's very common. The poor plant, banished suddenly from the cozy warmth in the room, goes into shock. It gets droopy, its leaves may go brown or black at the tips—and it often won't recover.

If you have drapes at your windows, always tuck them behind plants during the winter months (ditto if you use blinds). Better still, keep tropical plants away from window ledges if you live in an area that's cursed with long, cold winters.

... And then the humidity

Humidity is crucial for houseplants, but the word is often misunderstood. Many beginners assume that if their plants are watered long enough—and regularly enough—their plants will get enough humidity. Unfortunately, that's not the case. The term "humidity" means the relative amount of water vapor contained in the air. It has nothing to do how wet you keep your plant's containers.

Why plants need that moisture

The leaves of all plants are covered in stomata (tiny pores) that open to receive gases in the atmosphere. When the stomata open, the leaves lose moisture, in a process called transpiration. If there isn't sufficient water vapor in the air to accommodate for this loss, the leaves get parched. They may shrivel. The buds (and/or flowers) may fall off. The whole plant will fade. This can happen remarkably quickly in buildings that are centrally heated.

Scientists measure the amount of moisture in the air through what's called the "relative humidity factor." A factor of 100% equals fog—you can actually see the droplets of moisture under those conditions. Most houseplants don't need to spend their lives drenched in this kind of foggy mist. A humidity factor of around 40% will keep them happily churning out juicy green leaves. (Some specimens that come from steamy tropical jungles do prefer the air to be practically dripping with moisture, but they're the kind of plants you see growing in greenhouses.)

Generally speaking, houseplants with thick, leathery leaves are better able to withstand the winter dryness in our homes because they lose less moisture to transpiration. But all plants prefer some humidity. To ensure there's enough water vapor in the air to keep your plants healthy and happy,

Do

✓ Buy a humidifier. It's the best way to make sure houseplants stay fresh and green. Small table-top models that vaporize water (such as Pure Mist) are terrific if you live in

Spraying a fine mist of water over plants helps keep humidity high—and costs peanuts. Pick up a cheap plastic misting bottle at a hardware store (you can find fancier models at garden decor boutiques, but the cheapies work just as well). Spray daily, directly onto the foliage and flowers. Make sure the water's clean. Don't let it go stagnant in the bottle.

a small space. Drum humidifiers are a good choice in large homes because they circulate moisture to a wider area.

✓ Ask to see a demonstration of the humidifier before buying it. Some models are much noisier than others.

✓ Run the humidifier for a few hours every day of the year if you live in a contained environment that's heated in winter and air-conditioned in summer.

✓ Put it in the same room as the majority of your houseplants.

✓ Make sure the unit is in an accessible spot and can be filled easily. (You don't want to be slopping water all over the floor.)

✓ Put saucers under your plants, filled with half an inch (1.25 cm) of water.

✓ Raise the plants up in the saucers, on a layer of pebbles.

✓ Put several plants together on a tray, with pebbles underneath them. Grouping the leaves together helps the plants retain humidity.

Don't

✗ Forget to fill the humidifier. They run out of water awfully quickly!

✗ Leave water to get stagnant in plant saucers. It should be changed regularly.

✗ Buy tropical plants that have thin, papery leaves, such as caladiums, if the humidity in your home is low. Generally speaking, these need more moisture than the kinds with thick, strappy greenery.

Hot tip

"Put your humidifier in an unobtrusive spot, like behind the sofa, and run it every night. I turn mine on at 8:30 p.m., then turn it off when I get up. My plants love it."
—*Richard Tawton,*
condo houseplant fan

Potting and Fertilizing

Most indoor plants have one big advantage over plants bought for the outdoor garden: they don't have to be planted. Not initially, anyway. Whether you bring home a strapping ficus tree or a tiny cactus, it usually comes potted up in its own container. Eventually, however, most houseplants need to be repotted into bigger pots as their roots take up more and more space. The growing mix also gets tired and starts to disappear (yes, really. It actually does turn into dust).

How to tell when a plant is pot-bound

A plant that's pot-bound is like a kid wearing shoes that are too small. Its "toes" get pinched, and eventually the whole plant may become permanently deformed or stunted. This is a very common occurrence. People often call up gardening hot lines to complain that there's "something wrong" with their indoor plants; on investigation, it turns out to be not insects or a viral infection (as the callers expect), but simply a case of the plants getting too big for their boots. A plant may be pot-bound if

- ❁ it's wilting—and doesn't perk up when you water it;
- ❁ leaf tips are turning brown;
- ❁ leaves are constantly turning yellow and dropping off (though this might also be caused by other factors, such as inconsistent watering (see page 112), or moving the plant);

✽ the leaves seem to be shrinking;

✽ water doesn't soak into the soil but runs over the top and down the sides of the container;

✽ roots are poking out the drainage holes at the bottom.

Repotting the wise way

Do

✓ Water the pot-bound plant about an hour before you plan to give it a new home; the roots will be less inclined to be brittle—and break.

✓ Lay newspaper on the floor for easy cleanup.

✓ Turn the pot upside down and, cradling the plant in your hand, knock the pot against the side of a table. This should loosen the root ball. (It may take a few raps.)

✓ With big pots, run a knife blade around the soil ball to loosen it, then enlist the help of a friend to tip the plant out. If the plant won't come loose, you may be forced to break the container open (let's hope it's a cheap plastic one).

✓ Lift out the root ball and inspect it.

✓ If roots are entangled in crockery at the bottom of the pot, loosen them gently.

✓ Check for bugs (particularly mealy bugs) and cut off diseased or mushy-looking bits. If the plant is full of creepy-crawlies, throw it out.

✓ Choose the same kind of pot as before for the plant's new home. Plants are like people: they don't like drastic change foisted upon them. If the plant was growing in a plastic pot, don't switch to clay—and vice versa.

✓ Put crockery, stones, or a coffee filter in the bottom of the new container.

✓ Add some growing mix or potting soil, pushing it up the pot sides a bit. Then position the root ball on top. Aim to have at least half an inch (1.25 cm) of space between the top of the soil and the rim of the pot so soil won't run over the sides of the pot when you water.

> **Hot tip**
>
> "I think plants do best in clay pots. It has to do with moisture absorption—kind of like your socks, only not quite so pungent."
> —David Eddy, houseplant lover

✓ Pack more soil around the root ball with your fingers. Push it in firmly.

✓ Thump the pot on the table as you're doing this. It helps the soil settle in the pot.

✓ Have lots more soil on hand than you think you'll need. Running out halfway through the job is annoying (and often happens).

✓ Water the plant thoroughly as soon as you have finished repotting.

Don't

✗ Yank plants out of pots by their leaves and stems.

✗ Use a pot that's too big. It's tempting to repot a plant in a huge container to save the task of doing it again down the road. But most plants prefer to "move up" slowly. Generally speaking, there should be about an inch (2.5 cm) of air space between the plant's root ball and the sides of the new container

✗ Use old, grubby pots, with soil clinging to their interiors. Wash used pots thoroughly (see below).

✗ Press the plant down with your hands if it's sitting too high in the pot. The roots will get compressed. Instead, remove the plant from the pot and start again.

Hot tip

"Raid your kitchen cabinet for houseplant tools, or go to garage sales. You don't need to buy anything expensive. An old stock pot is great for mixing up potting soil. Stir it with an old fork. Dole the soil into pots with an old kitchen spoon. Use a chopstick to make holes for plant cuttings."
—*Mary-Fran McQuade, budget gardener*

Wash your pots

Anytime you use an old pot, scrub it out first to prevent diseases and bug eggs that may have been lurking in the pot from infecting your plant. Mix water with a bit of bleach—a cupful (250 mL) to a bucket or sinkful of water is a good ratio—and wear rubber gloves. (Long gloves that reach above the elbows are perfect for this job. They're sold in hardware stores, or by mail order from garden products companies.) Remove hardened bits of soil and decayed matter clinging to the sides of pots with a hard brush. Rinse the pots and let them dry before filling them with growing mix.

Potting soil or soil-less mix?

Those big, shiny bags at garden centers can be bewildering. It's hard to know which product to buy. Check the labels; there are now special formulas for many different kinds of plants—African violets, cactus, and orchids, for example—and it pays to pick an appropriate one. But bear in mind that the most expensive mix isn't necessarily the best. A garden writer who conducted tests found that mixes varied enormously, and in one test (on annual plants grown in window boxes) the most expensive mix performed the worst.

Potting soil: Also sometimes called houseplant soil, potting soil is heavier than growing mixes, and it works well for most houseplants. If you're repotting a big plant, pick potting soil instead of a lightweight growing mix—it will anchor the plant better.

Bagged potting soil varies enormously, but usually contains a mixture of organic and inorganic ingredients such as peat moss, compost, sand, and vermiculite. Some products have slow-release fertilizers added. You'll also see "sterilized" potting soil, which has been heated to over 180°F (82°C) to kill bacteria and weed seeds. It's fine to use this, particularly if you're worried about bugs and bacteria multiplying indoors. However, *don't* buy sterilized soil if you intend to stick to organic fertilizers, such as fish emulsion or seaweed extract. These products need the microorganisms found in the unsterilized stuff to work.

Don't start seeds in potting soil (it's too heavy), and never bring soil from the garden indoors—it may be full of bugs, which will multiply like mad in your pots.

Soil-less mixes: Lighter than potting soil, soil-less mixes are specially formulated for plants grown in containers. They usually consist of peat moss (lots of it), plus perlite and/or vermiculite, both of which look like nubbly bits of Styrofoam. Other organic materials, such as composted softwood bark, may be added, as well as slow-release fertilizers. The additives are all designed to improve drainage.

Most potted plants require good drainage. The best way to supply it is to add sand to your growing mix. Cacti crave a high proportion of sand. Herbs also seem to thrive in soil that's on the sandy side. You can sometimes find bags labeled "horticultural sand" at garden centers. But it's much cheaper to buy regular builder's sand at a home reno store or a construction site. Do not use beach sand from the ocean (it's too salty) or fine sand from around a lake. It should feel coarse and contain sharp particles. (Gardening books often use the rather mystifying term "sharp sand" to describe this stuff.)

Some of these mixes are "sterilized," some aren't. Both work fine, but the same rules regarding fertilizers apply to mixes as to potting soil. If you want to "go organic," don't selected a sterilized mix. Starting seeds is another matter. You *must* use a sterile mix (see page 71).

Generally speaking, short-lived flowering plants do better in a lightweight mix than in potting soil. But shop around and experiment, because the contents of those bags you see at garden centers can be very unpredictable.

Cheer your plants with charcoal

Add a small chunk of charcoal to your growing mix—it will help absorb odors and other impurities, such as fertilizer salts. It's especially good in the bottom of a container that has no drainage—an aquarium or a bottle, for instance. Charcoal can be hard to find in garden centers. Buy it at a pet store, where it's sold for use in aquarium filters.

A few fertilizer facts

The topic of fertilizers perplexes many people. Those funny groups of numbers—15-30-15, 20-20-20—what do they mean? Is it necessary to know all this scientific stuff?

No—and yes. Amateur indoor gardeners don't need to understand the complex technical aspects of fertilizers and how they work. But a basic understanding of plant nutrients (which is what fertilizers are) is helpful, because your potted plants require them to thrive. The fact is, most plants grown in containers do better if they receive occasional applications of fertilizer. This may pose an ethical dilemma if you're concerned about the environment (nowadays, many of us hesitate to do anything "artificial"), but there simply isn't sufficient nourishment in containers to leave everything to Mother Nature in the long term.

What the numbers mean

All fertilizers contain three basic nutrients:

- Nitrogen (N) promotes growth of green leaves and stems.
- Phosphorus (P) helps roots, flowers, and fruit grow.
- Potassium (K) assists flowering and fruiting, but also helps plants develop strong stems and resistance to disease.

The three symbols are always listed in that order on product labels. A bottle of plant food that says 5-10-5 on its label contains 5% nitrogen, 10% phosphorus, and 5% potassium.

What's best to use? It depends on your plants. A good all-round formula is 20-20-20 or 10-10-10. These work well with most houseplants.

Organic or chemical?

Both have merits. "Natural" fertilizers—often, composted manure, fish emulsion, bone meal, and/or blood meal—are more expensive, but they take effect slowly and generally won't harm plants. Chemical products get quicker results, but can burn leaves and roots if used incorrectly. Ultimately, the choice is a personal one. Look for a product that suits what you're growing and follow label instructions to the letter. More plants are killed by people being too generous with fertilizer than by anything else.

Caution: don't use organic fertilizers containing fish emulsion or blood meal if you have cats. Kitties are attracted to the smell of both, and the little devils will often dig up potted plants in search of a snack. The same rule applies if you live in an area that's plagued by raccoons and you plan to put your plants outside on a balcony or deck in summertime. These wild critters love blood meal and things that smell fishy, and they will go digging too.

Hot tip

"I don't fertilize my houseplants at all in winter. That's when they're sleeping. And at other times of the year, I only fertilize once every two months. You shouldn't overdo fertilizer."

—*Richard Tawton, houseplant lover*

Wet or dry?

There are many different fertilizers aimed at home gardeners nowadays. They have names like Granny's Jungle Juice and Bob's Therapy for Houseplants, and are divided into five basic types:

🏵 **Liquid:** Some of these you mix into a watering can, others are ready to use, and you spray them directly on leaves or the soil. The latter may be called "foliar spray" or "nutritional spray" or "nutrient leaf spray" or simply "plant food." Sprays are certainly easy to use. However, they have drawbacks. It's easy to overdo the spraying by mistake, burning leaves, and the nutrients are quickly leached from the soil when you water the plant. Use them with caution. Most foliar sprays are designed to give a quick boost to plants that are looking lousy. Organic liquid fertilizers, such as seaweed extract (also called kelp), which you dilute with water, are a better bet. They won't burn plants and are a good source of micronutrients. But they tend to be expensive.

🏵 **Soluble:** These usually come in the form of crystals (often a lurid shade of turquoise), which you mix into a jug of water. They are the most widely used fertilizers for potted plants, and are often simply labeled "plant food." You will see different concentrations, but 20-20-20 is a good all-round formula that works well for most houseplants. Use this stuff sparingly; don't be tempted to mix more crystals into your watering can than the directions indicate. And let the concoction sit overnight before you pour it on plants.

🏵 **Spikes:** Little stakes of compacted fiber, impregnated with fertilizer, that you push into the soil. They are convenient for houseplants, but be sure to pick the right size or you may burn the plants' roots. Spikes also tend to be expensive. Soluble fertilizers give a bigger bang for the buck.

❀ **Teabags:** A new gimmick that's becoming hot. Basically, this is composted manure packed in "teabags" and sold in a pretty box. You soak the bags for twenty-four hours in water, then pour on plants. One product is called Barnyard Bounty. It's 100% organic and won't harm plants, but its nutrient concentration is very weak—only 2-3-2—and so it won't deliver much of a boost.

❀ **Time-release:** Fertilizers in capsule form, just like the vitamins we take. These release nutrients over an extended period of time, usually up to nine months—and they are designed to work their magic as the soil temperature rises. They are better used outdoors than on indoor plants.

Wise Up to Watering

Worried about when to water your houseplants? You're not alone. Gauging the right time to give indoor plants a drink is a justifiable source of anxiety, because it's unquestionably more complicated than doing the job outdoors. In a garden or on a balcony, it's usually a simple matter of hauling out the garden hose or watering can when plants (or the lawn) look thirsty. However, in the artificial environment of our homes, watering is not so straightforward.

Five factors to consider

1. **What kind of plant is it?** Generally speaking, the thicker the leaves, the less water the plant needs (because it can store moisture in the foliage). A rubber plant, for instance, is virtually indestructible. But thin-leafed tropical plants such as caladiums require more TLC. Most should be kept slightly moist, but not water-logged. Some, like *Ficus benjamina*, must never be allowed to dry out. Their thin, shiny leaves are incapable of retaining water. (Finicky ficus may die abruptly, with no warning signs like wilting, if you forget to water it.) Most cacti and succulent plants prefer their soil on the dry side. So do flowering plants, such as kalanchoe, once their period of vigorous growth and flowering is finished. Other bloomers, such as amaryllis and spring bulbs, shouldn't receive much water when they're in bloom. Confusing, isn't it?

2. **Where is the plant growing?** In a sunny window, plants will dry out much more quickly than in the interior of a room. They'll stay damp in a bathroom or kitchen. If the room is very warm, with the central heating going full blast, they'll probably require more frequent watering than what's considered normal for those types of plants. The proximity of heating and air-conditioning ducts, radiators, and fireplaces also plays a big role.

3. **What season is it?** During the winter, most plants have a slower rate of growth, so they require less water. Some go into semi-hibernation and need only a dribble of water now and then to stay alive. Most plants are at their thirstiest in spring, when they're putting out lots of fresh new growth, and summer. But there are exceptions. Winter-blooming tuberous plants, such as cyclamens, require plenty of water in winter, but none in summer, when they go dormant.

4. **What type of pots and growing mix have you used?** Pot up two identical houseplants indoors—one in a clay flowerpot, the other in plastic. You'll be amazed by how much quicker the clay container dries out. Growing mixes also influence how often you need to water. Potting soil retains water much longer than mixes containing peat moss, vermiculite, or perlite. If you add sand to your mix (a smart idea with some plants, like cacti and spring bulbs, that like good drainage) the pot will dry out faster.

5. **How old are your plants?** Plants that are established, with lots of roots twirling around inside their pots, need water more often than new plants.

> ## Hot tip
> "Choose a particular day of the week to water your plants. Then attach a word to that day to remind you. For instance, Moisten Monday or Wet Wednesday or Thirsty Thursday. That way, you won't forget."
> —*Anne Lockley, houseplant lover*

Check plant labels

Take the trouble to examine the information shown on plant labels; they usually provide the best guide to a plant's watering requirements. (But remember to take the factors listed above into consideration.) Look for one of three magic words on the label:

🌸 "Plentifully," or "frequently," means you should keep the growing mix consistently moist. Never let it dry out.

🌸 "Moderately" means give the plant a good soak, but let the top inch (2.5 cm) or so of the mix dry out before you water again.

🌸 "Sparingly" indicates that only an occasional watering is required. Never soak the plant so that water comes out the bottom of the pot. Let the growing mix get dry as a bone before watering again.

If the leaves wilt or the entire plant gets droopy, you're not watering enough. Some plants' stems may shrink, as well. But sometimes there are no warning signs. The plant will simply shrivel up and die from lack of water.

Overwatering: It's the biggest mistake beginners can make

We're so keen to cosset our plants, we often give the poor things too much to drink—and they drown. Plants will sometimes wilt when there's insufficient water, but this condition is also an indicator that you are wielding the watering can too often. Other telltale signs are leaves turning yellow, stems that are soft and transparent-looking (or turning black), and soil that is sodden, not simply moist. Turn an unhappy-looking plant out of its pot and examine its roots. If they look mushy and black, you're giving it too much water. Cut the mushy bits off and restore the plant to its pot with some fresh growing mix. It may recover.

Another common mistake is inconsistent watering. Most plants prefer a regimen. Yellow leaves are often a sign that your watering practices are not consistent enough. Put your plants on a schedule and stick to it. If you water once a week, for example, always water on the same day.

> **Hot tip**
> "If your houseplants are looking waterlogged, wrap a pencil in a piece of newspaper and insert it in the soil. The newspaper will absorb the water."
> —*Deirdre Black, houseplant lover*

Who watered the broadloom?

You can always tell the homes of houseplant addicts: they're the ones with water marks on the coffee tables and stained patches on the carpet or hardwood flooring. But these folks aren't just sloppy. It's awfully easy to make a mess when watering plants indoors. Water comes out the drainage hole at the bottom, overflows from the saucer, and oops!

Here's how to give plants a drink without wrecking everything else in the process:

Do

✓ Buy a watering can that's designed for houseplants. It should have a long, slim curving spout that pokes right into pots—and it should not be too big. It's courting disaster to lug around heavy containers full of water.

✓ Aim the water at the soil, not the leaves.

✓ Move small plants to the kitchen sink or bathtub to water them.

✓ Make sure the saucers underneath pots are deep enough to hold the runoff.

✓ Place a layer of gravel in saucers to raise houseplants up, providing more space for the runoff.

> **Hot tip**
>
> "Plastic dinner trays sold at restaurant and hotel supply stores are great for putting underneath indoor plants. Spread a thin layer of aquarium gravel on the tray, then group plants together, without saucers, on top of the gravel."
>
> —*Priscilla Leung, houseplant fan*

✓ Water from the bottom, if you can, by filling the saucer and letting the plant drink up the water through its roots. For some hairy-leaved plants, like African violets, this is a must. Check plant labels.

✓ Be careful of potted plants crammed too full of soil. Spring bulbs are often sold this way. When you water, the overflow will dribble down the sides. There should be at least half an inch (1.25 cm) of space between the top of the soil and the pot rim.

✓ Do messy jobs—like mixing plant food into watering cans, or repotting plants—at the kitchen or bathroom sink, not on the dining room table.

Don't

✗ Use an outdoor watering can with a rose nozzle. It will spray water everywhere.

✗ Leave plants sitting in saucers of water and then keep adding more water on top. This will rot the roots of many plants. Tip the residue out after a few hours, or if that's not practical (as with big pots), suck it out with a turkey baster.

✗ Pour water onto long, pointy leaves that have an indentation running down their centers (those of amaryllis, for instance). The water will run straight down those leaves onto the floor.

✗ Leave decorative wrap around potted plants. It's not waterproof. Take the foil off (it looks tacky, anyway) and stand the pot in a saucer before you water.

Lukewarm is luverly

Most plants don't like being subjected to an icy cold shower any more than we do. Fill your watering can and let it sit overnight before giving plants a drink. Here's another advantage of waiting a while before watering: chlorine (which plants hate) gets dispelled from city tap water if it's allowed to sit in a container for a few hours. If you have lots of plants to water, keep a bucket handy under the sink or in the bath, then dip into that with an old yogurt container.

Gadgets and gizmos to water with

All kinds of gadgets are available now. Some are terrific, others a waste of money. Look for these in mail-order garden supply catalogs:

❀ **Telescoping hoses:** They look like concertinaed telephone cords and thus don't take up much space. You can attach them to a kitchen tap and stash them in a cupboard after use.

🏵 **The RainStick:** If you have lots of hanging baskets, this gadget—which is basically an oversized syringe—will be a godsend. Draw water from a bucket or kitchen sink into the syringe, then squirt it into the center of the plant. It's ideal for use indoors because you can direct the water where it's needed most, without splashing everything else.

🏵 **Automatic plant waterers:** The best ones come from Europe and are designed specifically for use with indoor plants. They have ceramic cones with lids, which are inserted into potting mix and connected to thin hoses plunked into jars of water. You fill the cone and the jar with water. More liquid is wicked through the hose as the plant needs it. They are effective, but you can get the same effect with a homemade wicking system.

How to wick water into plants

It's a smart idea to provide all plants with a wicking system when you plant them, in case you go away. Then you can simply stick the wick into a container of water during your absence. Here's a method that works:

🏵 Buy some 3-ply synthetic knitting yarn. Don't use wool (it rots). Old pantyhose, cut into pieces, or nylon cord from a fishing supply store are also fine.

🏵 Thread a long piece of yarn through the hole in the pot before you add growing mix. Then fill the pot with mix, making sure to leave a short length of yarn sticking out of the bottom and a longer piece hanging over the pot's side.

🏵 When you've filled the pot and positioned the plant in it, cut off the length of yarn sticking out the bottom.

✾ To wick water, simply place the long end of the yarn sticking out at the top into a water-filled container. (Put it in an unobtrusive spot, behind the pot. Strings of yarn and old pantyhose aren't exactly elegant.) Old cottage cheese tubs make good containers. Cut a hole in their lids. You can also give plants a gentle dose of fertilizer using this wicking system. Just mix the plant food crystals into the water container.

Get out the DustBuster

We've all been in homes full of dusty houseplants. Aside from being unattractive, dust isn't good for the plants—it prevents them from breathing. Wash your greenery regularly, and it will be healthier. The simplest method is to occasionally put your plants under the shower. If they're too big to haul into the bathroom, treat them to a sponge bath. Wipe leaves off with a damp cloth or sponge, dipped in clean water. Be sure to support big leaves with one hand while you wipe with the other. Wipe the undersides of leaves, too.

Some people swear by olive oil or beer to clean houseplant leaves. Others think milk is marvelous. Still others buy commercial leaf-shine products. The truth is, a glossy leaf isn't necessarily a healthy one. Plain, lukewarm water works best. Some of the other substances may make plants shine, but they block their pores and often leave residue on the leaves. Milk and beer may also turn sour and get smelly.

When you go on vacation

Group plants in the bathtub or kitchen sink, give them a shower before you go, and then leave them there. And stop worrying. Most indoor plants will survive well in that setup for a couple of weeks. For longer absences,

❀ Drape a length of self-wicking mat (sold at garden centers) on the kitchen counter, with one end of the mat dipped into a sink full of water. Stand pots on the counter, with the mat underneath them. Water will wick upwards by capillary action. Alternatively, use the homemade wicking system described above.

❀ Put transparent plastic bags over moisture-loving plants and seal them closed with elastics. (Be careful not to crush foliage when you do this. Use big bags.)

❀ Ask someone who knows about plants to come in and water for you. *Occasionally.* One of the biggest complaints of indoor gardeners is that, when they go away, well-meaning friends promptly kill their house-plants by overwatering them.

Mites, Mildew, and Other Nasties

We live in a buggy world, and there's no escaping it inside our homes. In fact, houseplants are quite vulnerable to attack by all kinds of infuriating insects and creepy-crawlies, partly because they live in what is essentially an artificial environment. Bugs may hitch a ride indoors on one plant, then multiply like mad on neighboring plants if the conditions are right. And unlike their cousins ensconced out of doors, these imported bugs don't get killed off in winter. It's pretty much the same story with viruses and fungal diseases. They may take hold and become hard to eradicate.

Another annoying fact of indoor gardening life is that most of the bugs that affect houseplants are tiny. So tiny you can't see the darn things without a magnifying glass. By the time you've noticed that something is laying siege to your poor peace lily, the culprit has had a chance to inflict major injury.

To keep infestations to a minimum,

- be meticulous about plant housekeeping (see page 116);
- make sure you maintain high humidity (see page 100);
- treat all your plants to the watering routine that fits their particular requirements (see page 110).

What are those disgusting things, anyway?

Aphids
Nasty little suckers (also called, appropriately, plant lice), aphids are the curse of gardeners everywhere. If they attack

your houseplants, be consoled: they inflict far more damage outside, in gardens. Aphids multiply rapidly and are cunning. They often change their colors like chameleons to match the plant they've chosen to munch on. However, their appearance hardly matters, because these trespassers are so small, you can't usually see them with the naked eye.

The telltale signs of an artillery attack by aphids are:

- stems, leaves, or flowers that suddenly go limp or get sticky;
- leaves that become puckered up, like pursed lips;
- white blobs (like spittle) clinging to the plant;
- whitish "skeletons" (aphids' outer skins, which they shed and regrow regularly as they go about their business).

Aphids can affect virtually anything grown indoors, but they are particularly partial to hibiscus, dieffenbachias, ivies (*Hedera*), hoyas, and basil.

Fungus gnats

These are little flies, a bit like miniature daddy-long-legs. They start out as larvae in potting soil. In most instances, you'll see a lot of them suddenly start appearing from nowhere (in reality, they're hatching out in your pots), then flying about the room. Fungus gnats are annoying, but they usually don't harm plants, although one kind can damage roots. They can appear in virtually any potted plant, but bulbs, geraniums, and poinsettia are particularly vulnerable. To avoid them, use sterile soil-less mix.

Mealy bugs

These fall into the "crawler" category. They don't fly, and they usually cluster on stems and leaves, or in leaf axils or roots, sucking the life blood out of plants. Mealy bugs' only good attribute is that you can actually spot them: they're oval, about an eighth of an inch (0.3 cm) long, with spiky bits sticking out all around their nasty little bodies. But they are often hidden (like spider mites) under a white, woolly overcoat that they spin. One telltale sign of mealy bugs is honeydew

dripping from plants. Other pointers are leaves turning yellow or the whole plant withering.

Mealy bugs enjoy munching on African violets, amaryllis, begonias, clivias, coleus, dracaenas, dieffenbachias, epipremnums, ficuses, hoyas, scheffleras, syngoniums, and various cacti and orchids.

What honeydew is

In the supermarket it's a tasty melon. But for houseplants it's not so nice. "Honeydew" is the rather inappropriate word that garden experts use to describe the stuff bugs secrete while sucking the sap out of plants. It's yellowish, orangey, or clear, and sticky. If you see blobs of honeydew on the floor or table where your plants are, or a liquidy substance dripping from leaves or flowers, the plant is under attack. It could be aphids, mealy bugs, scale, or whiteflies. Whatever the culprit is, act fast.

Red spider mites

Like most bugs, these start out on the undersides of leaves. But they can multiply—and move around—at an incredible rate, especially in hot, dry air. One condo gardener (who bought a lot of houseplants for her solarium but neglected to install a humidifier) wound up with spider mites in her sofa, her bed, and even, to her horror, in her nightdress. It took months of repeatedly washing everything in her unit to get rid of them.

Spider mites are pink or red, and so small you probably won't notice them. What you do see, however, is their webs. These are a whitish weaving (or coating) mostly on the undersides of leaves, but also on leaf tops or clinging to the stems. In bad infestations, these webs will wrap themselves around entire section of plants, distorting their appearance. Other telltale signs are "webby" foliage that has turned pale, or leaf tips that are stippled with dots, or twisted.

Organic solutions to spider mites abound because they are the number one problem plaguing houseplants. Old timers recommend this concoction: mix half a cup (125 mL) of buttermilk with 4 cups (1 L) of wheat flour, then stir this paste into a bucket containing 5 gallons (19 L) of water. Immerse the entire pot, plant and all, in the bucket. You can also spray or paint this gluey substance on stems and leaves. It is supposed to work by suffocating the mites and killing their eggs.

Plants that are particularly prone to red spider mites are African violets, azaleas, crotons, cyclamen, dieffenbachias, dracaenas, hibiscus, marantas, many ivies (*Hedera*), and palms.

Scale

Scale isn't crud found inside the kettle. It's alive: a horrid insect, with a hard, horny casing, that sucks sap from stems. If there's honeydew dripping from plants and their leaves are turning yellow and dropping, the problem could be scale. When mature, these brownish or yellowish invaders encase themselves completely in a waxy suit of armor that coats entire stems of plants and is difficult to remove.

Scale typically affects bay trees, citrus trees, euonymus, ferns (but don't mistake ferns' spore-bearing organs for scale; they look similar), ficuses, jasmine, and various orchids and palms.

> **Hot tip**
> "Houseplant bugs can't swim. If you submerge your plants in a tub of lukewarm water, the bugs will drown."
> —*Charlie Dobbin, houseplant expert*

Whiteflies

If a cloud of insects rises from a houseplant when you touch it, it's probably whiteflies. These have pale, shimmery wings, and they cluster in vast numbers on the tops and undersides of leaves, where they lay larvae (which are greenish or transparent). Whiteflies suck sap from plants and excrete honeydew. The entire plant will eventually wilt.

Flowering plants are often affected by whiteflies. Their favorite victims are geraniums of all kinds and fuchsias.

How to battle the bug brigade safely

Gardening books—old and new—often advocate using a bewildering arsenal of chemical weapons against bugs and viral diseases on houseplants. But many of these pesticides—which have names like Chlorobenzilate, Diazinon, and Lindane—have been proven to be highly toxic to humans and pets. A few, such as Diazinon, have already been banned for use in gardens in certain municipalities. Who wants to have such products sitting around at home or sprayed into the air we breathe indoors? Not sensible gardeners, surely.

When bugs attack, try an environmentally-friendly way of getting rid of them first. Use pesticides only as a last resort. Organic methods are usually more fiddly than zapping nuisances with a shot of something lethal—and they take persistence. But they can work. Here are some tips:

Do

✓ Be careful where you buy plants. Avoid "fly by night" operations, which are often set up at roadsides during the summer. The plants sold in these temporary garden centers may be cheap, but they don't receive proper care—and they may have been acquired from dubious sources.

✓ When repotting plants, always use sterile mix (see page 105).

✓ Isolate plants immediately if you suspect something is wrong.

✓ Keep a magnifying glass on hand to examine plants. Turn leaves and pots upside down if you can. Pay particular attention to the undersides of leaves.

✓ If you detect insects, dunk the plant in a bucket of lukewarm soapy water. Immerse the entire plant, pot and all. Then rinse. Repeat this procedure three days later, then again ten days later.

✓ If only one stem of a plant is buggy, cut it off. Throw it away immediately, wrapped in a plastic bag. Then do the soap and water routine with the rest of the plant.

✓ Spray the soapy water on affected areas with a misting bottle if the plant is too big for the "dunk" approach.

✓ If you have a sprayer with your kitchen faucet, give the undersides of leaves a blast. This may wash bugs off.

✓ Dab individual insects that you can see (like mites and scale) with a Q-tip dipped in isopropryl alcohol. Watch them squirm—and feel triumphant.

✓ Scrape scale off stems with a fingernail or the blunt edge of a knife, if you can bear it. (It's yucky—and you have to be careful not to damage the stems.)

It's not necessary to buy expensive insecticidal soaps to wash plants. A mild dishwashing liquid such as Ivory will do the job just as well. But don't use detergent. Just put a few squirts of dishwashing liquid into a full sink (or pail) of lukewarm water, then immerse plants, pots and all. Be sure to rinse them thoroughly.

✓ Put infected plants in a see-through plastic bag. Seal the bag. Check again in a couple of weeks. If the bugs are back, consider getting rid of the plant.

✓ Sprinkle a bit of tobacco on the tops of pots. We all know how harmful nicotine can be to humans. It sometimes kills bugs too.

✓ With white fly infestations, buy a yellow sticky strip (sold at garden centers) and put it in a plastic bag, along with the plant. The flies will—you hope—get stuck on the strip.

Don't

✗ Try to salvage a badly infected plant. Throw it out. And if bugs or disease problems keep coming back, give all your plants the heave-ho and start again.

✗ Allow a new arrival to join your plant collection right away. Keep it separate for a few weeks until you're sure it's in good shape.

What is guttation?

Sometimes, honeydew isn't caused by insects, but by a curious phenomenon called "guttation," which occurs with some houseplants when they are watered incorrectly. Liquid starts dripping from the tips of their leaves, and it may feel sticky. Dieffenbachia is particularly susceptible. So is ficus. You can trigger guttation by allowing plants to completely dry out and then watering them too heavily. To find out if that's the problem, examine the leaves carefully. You should see white droplets of latex, especially on the main vein (and, of course, there won't be any bugs evident on the plant). To remedy the problem, don't let the plant get bone dry between waterings. Keep the soil a bit moist.

✗ Don't bring houseplants indoors in fall without giving them a bath first (see page 129). There's a barrelful of bugs lurking out there in the great green world. Bugs (and bug eggs) hitchhiking a ride indoors, once the cold weather comes, are the most common cause of infestations on houseplants during the winter.

When plants look sick—but you don't see any bugs

The problem could be an infection or viral disease. These can affect any part of indoor plants—leaves, stems, flowers, or roots—and they are bad news because they can spread quickly to other plants. There are also no satisfactory treatments for many of these afflictions. Often, the best bet is to throw the affected plant out. The most common problems are:

- **Black leg:** The name fits because stems go black and rot at the base. It's mostly caused by overwatering.
- **Botrytis:** Leaves and stems develop a fluffy, raised, gray mold. It happens when the humidity is too high, and usually affects plants with soft leaves and stems (like coleus).
- **Leaf spot:** Brownish or yellowish blotches, often with damp centers, appear on leaves. These patches keep spreading and may eventually meet up. Or they become hard and brownish.
- **Powdery mildew:** This very common mildew is much whiter in appearance than botrytis mold and not as "fluffy." It often affects rosemary bushes brought indoors for the winter.
- **Stem and crown rot:** This looks very similar to black leg. The decaying part usually gets horribly slimy and soft.
- **Weird viruses with no name:** Humans get them. Unfortunately, so do plants. The symptoms may be anything from yellow streaking and mottling of leaves to distortion or stunting of the whole plant.

How to deter plant diseases

- Be careful about overwatering. It's one of the most common causes of disease. Soil shouldn't get soggy. Avoid letting water settle on leaves, and don't be a maniac with the misting bottle.
- Don't crowd plants too tightly together. Mildew often sets in when there's insufficient space between plants.
- Avoid damaging plants, or breaking stems, when you handle them. That's an invitation to infection.
- Set up a little fan close to plants and leave it on for a few hours a day to circulate the air.
- If you suspect a virus, cut the affected part of the plant off, using a sharp, clean knife, and move it to another room. If the problem keeps returning, throw the plant out.
- Avoid handling healthy plants after you've been tending to a sick one. Wash your hands first.
- Try treating mildew and leaf spot with baking soda. Mix a teaspoonful (5 mL) into a misting bottle and spray on plants. Repeat at three-day intervals. This sometimes helps—but you have to keep doing it again and again to get results.

Hot tip

"Spraying the undersides of houseplant leaves is always difficult. Try a misting bottle that's new on the market. Its nozzle is angled upwards, rather than downwards. I got mine from a company that sells garden products by mail—and I love it."

—*Gwen Farrow, condo gardener*

What To Do with Houseplants in the Summer

Should we put them outside? Leave them inside? Opinions differ strongly on this issue. Some experienced gardeners are vehement that houseplants should never go into a garden (or onto a deck or balcony) during the warm months. "It weakens the plants," argues one, "and it makes them vulnerable to infection—and attacks by insects." Other gardening experts are just as adamant that indoor plants benefit from a dose of fresh air. "After being cooped up indoors for the winter, houseplants like being outside as much as we do," says one nursery manager. "I always put mine out in the garden. They get lots of new growth, and that sets them up for the following fall, when I bring them indoors again."

Ultimately, it's a matter of personal choice. But if you are going to give your plants a summer vacation outdoors, it's important to break them into their new environment slowly. Houseplants are like residents of a northern city going off on a winter trip south. They've been used to low light levels inside, and suddenly they're plunked somewhere that's much brighter (light levels outside are invariably brighter than in our homes, even if we grow plants under lights). They may also have to cope with seesaw temperatures, wind, and rain. They need time to acclimatize or they'll get sunburned and out of sorts—and unlike humans, they may never recover from the shock.

> **Hot tip**
> "I always put my hibiscus and benjamina out of doors in summer, and by September they look fantastic."
> —*Mark Cullen,*
> *gardening show host*

Safe steps to take

Do

✓ Group plants together in a shady, sheltered spot in the garden (or on a balcony) where they won't receive *any* direct sunlight for at least a couple of weeks.

✓ Water all plants well after you put them outside.

✓ Be very careful about dappled shade. Tree leaves cast this kind of shade, and one problem with it is that it's not constant or impenetrable. The sun breaks through, particularly on a windy day when leaves are blowing to and fro, and it can be incredibly fierce. You may think you're giving houseplants a shady spot, but the reality is often different. The plants can actually get visible burn spots if piercing rays of sunlight sneak through the leaves.

✓ Whatever the location, if the indirect light is fierce, gently cover the plants with a light-colored sheet for the first week. This is particularly important if you've put them

If you've moved into a new condo and are strapped for cash, save money when summer comes by putting your houseplants outside on your balcony or terrace. The "tropical look" is all the rage nowadays in gardening—and that's exactly what many houseplants supply, in spades. Their big flamboyant leaves look great grouped together on a deck or balcony.

on a balcony high off the ground, where they'll be exposed to wind, as well.

✓ Keep houseplants that normally thrive in low-light conditions—such as philodendrons, Chinese evergreens, spathiphyllums, and spider plants—in a shady area all summer. The same goes for amaryllis and clivias.

✓ Move cacti, rosemary bushes, bay trees, geraniums, and succulents such as jade plants out into the sun after an adjustment period—but do it slowly. Expose them to the sun's rays for only an hour the first day, then gradually increase their exposure. (If you have a trolley to move the plants in and out of the sun, this makes the job easier.)

✓ Cut houseplants right back if they developed growth that's pale and leggy over the winter. So long as you keep them well watered and nourished with plant food, they'll usually develop fresh new leaves quickly.

Don't

✗ Leave a houseplant sitting in the sunshine if it's obviously wilting. Move it immediately to a shady spot.

✗ Forget to water plants. They need more water than usual after their introduction to the great outdoors.

When winter rolls around

We often slow down. So do our plants. Generally speaking, plants grow much more slowly in winter—in fact, some go as dormant as hibernating bears. Cacti, for instance, will actually shrink in winter. Even if they don't lose weight, most plants require less of everything: watering, fertilizing, overall fussing. In fact, many of them like to be left alone, with just a drizzle of water now and then to keep them alive.

If you're bringing houseplants back indoors after a summer spent outside, take a crucially important step: give them all a "plunge bath" in lukewarm soapy water. Here's how to do it:

🌸 Use a mild detergent such as Dove. Put a few squirts of it into the kitchen sink, the bathtub, or a bucket, mixed with lots of water.

🌸 Prune any dead or straggly bits off the plant, then plunge the whole thing into the bath, pot and all.

🌸 Immerse it for a few minutes, until bubbles have stopped coming to the surface.

🌸 Rinse the pot and plant off thoroughly (under the shower works well) and leave it outside to dry on a sunny fall day. Then bring it into its winter quarters (preferably a cool room at first, so it can adjust to being indoors).

Giving plants a bath gets rid of bugs that may be lurking, unnoticed, under the leaves. It also kill eggs that creepy-crawlies and flying insects might have laid in the soil—and it washes away fertilizer salts that have built up in the container during the summer. Experienced gardeners say scheduling a bath day is always worth the effort.

Hot tip

"Before giving houseplants a bath, pick up a special mesh strainer that fits over the drainage hole of sinks or bathtubs. It stops soil and plant debris getting washed down the drain. You can find these strainers at hardware stores. They're only a few dollars."
—Mary Wilkerson, condo houseplant fan

The Real Poop on Poisonous and Beneficial Houseplants

Can indoor plants kill us—or our kids and pets? Yes, it's undeniably possible, but the likelihood of this happening is *very* low. In fact, the poison potential of most houseplants is greatly exaggerated by the nervous Nellies of the world. In most instances, the benefits of having greenery around our homes far outweigh the drawbacks.

Which plants can harm us?

Some popular houseplants are definitely toxic, to varying degrees. They may make susceptible individuals sick with a variety of ailments ranging from stomach trouble to severe dermatitis. A few plants may also affect kids far more seriously than adults. And plants that don't bother humans can, in some cases, prompt poor Fido or Kitty to start barfing on the rug or showing other symptoms of poisoning. (Paradoxically, these problem plants often also do a good job of purifying the air. See page 134.) Here are common "baddies" to watch out for:

- **Aloe vera (*Aloe barbadensis*):** Often called the burn plant, this spiky, easy-to-grow tropical plant is a boon in the kitchen (see page 35). However, be sure to use only the jellified center of the aloe's "leaves," not the yellow juice that's immediately under its green skin. This liquidy stuff can give some people a bad rash. Note: use young plants. Older aloe plants contain lots of juice.
- **Amaryllis:** Don't ever mistake amaryllis bulbs for an exotic new onion. They cause diarrhea, nausea, and

vomiting (but you have to gobble down huge amounts of them to get sick).

🏵 **Angel's trumpet (*Datura arborea*):** This produces spectacular flowers, but if you have kids or pets, forget it. It's a relative of deadly Jimson weed (*Datura stramonium*) and shouldn't be grown indoors unless you're super careful. Sometimes called 'loco weed' because it makes cattle go crazy if they munch on it, *D. stramonium* is severely poisonous to humans and pets, and *D. arborea* is presumed to have similar effects. Symptoms include agitation, jerky movements, coma, drowsiness, hallucination, and elevated temperature.

🏵 **Azalea (*Rhododendron sp.*):** Classified as "low toxicity," azaleas should nonetheless be kept away from kids and pets. In fact, experts recommend treating all rhododendrons as poisonous.

🏵 **Caladiums:** If cats and dogs chew on these elegant houseplants with heart-shaped leaves, they'll get inflamed mouths and throats. Tummy upsets are another side effect.

🏵 **Castor bean plant (*Ricinus communis*):** This plant is so deadly poisonous, terrorists have been caught attempting to transform its seeds into biological weapons. Enough said.

🏵 **Crown of thorns (*Euphorbia milii*):** Many garden varieties of euphorbia exude an irritating sap. This one, often grown as a houseplant and sometimes called "Christ's thorn," is no exception. It can also cause abdominal pains and vomiting if eaten. Always wear garden gloves when handling euphorbias.

🏵 **Devil's backbone (*Kalanchoe daigremontiana*):** Also called "mother of thousands" because young plantlets grow along its leaf edges. These new "babies" are potential troublemakers, because toddlers and pets often pull them off the mother plant to have a nibble or play with them. That's not a good idea because leaves and stems are quite toxic and can cause death in rare instances. Be careful of all kalanchoes.

- **Devil's ivy (Pothos, *Epipremnum*, or *Scindapsus*):** There's no evidence that this easy-to-grow trailing plant is poisonous to humans, but some people say it causes dogs' and cats' lips and tongues to swell up if they chew on it.
- **Dieffenbachia:** This distinctively leafed plant is nicknamed "dumbcane" with good reason. Chew on it and you'll be struck dumb—a condition that can last for several days. (Fido's bark may be similarly zapped. Perhaps that's not such a bad thing.) The sap can also irritate skin.
- **English ivy (*Hedera helix*):** One of the most popular houseplants on the planet. But don't let pets nibble on its leaves or be tempted to use it as a garnish in cooking. Ingesting ivy may result in breathing difficulties, convulsions, paralysis, and coma. Some people also get a rash from the sap.
- **Flamingo lily (*Anthurium andraeanum*):** Sometimes called "painter's palette." Don't let pets play with this one or they'll get painful blistering of their mouths and throats. Further symptoms are gagging and difficulty breathing.
- **Hyacinth:** See page 86.

- **Hydrangea (*Hydrangea macrophylla*):** These shrubby garden plants are increasingly popular indoors. Eating the buds and leaves can cause vomiting, abdominal pains, diarrhea, lethargy, labored breathing, and coma. If you have sensitive skin, you may also get contact dermatitis when handling the plants.
- **Oleander (*Nerium*):** Increasingly popular as a houseplant in northern climates because of its pretty pink, red, white, or salmon flowers and graceful green-gray leaves, this shrub is so highly toxic, it's against the law to burn it on some Caribbean islands (oleander smoke can send susceptible individuals into convulsions). Don't let pets nibble on it, and avoid handling nerium with bare hands.

⚘ **Swiss cheese plant (*Monstera deliciosa*):**
Unfortunately, there's nothing delicious about this plant
(also called split-leaf philodendron). Its leaves are toxic to
both humans and pets. Symptoms include loss of speech,
blistering, hoarseness, mouth irritation, and raised watery
lesions on the skin, accompanied by intense itching.

How to avoid hassles with problem plants

Do

✓ Wear gloves when handling anything that
   may cause a rash.
✓ Group potentially hazardous houseplants
   together in a separate area of the house
   that's not accessible to family members
   and pets.
✓ Contact a doctor, go to the emergency
   department of a hospital, or call a vet if you
   suspect poisoning. Some people keep syrup
   of ipecac or hydrogen peroxide on hand
   and administer a dose to induce vomiting.

> ### Hot tip
> "Cats get neurotic if they're
> constantly told to stop nibbling
> on houseplants. So I let mine
> munch on my spider plant. It
> doesn't really hurt the plant,
> and it keeps the cats happy
> during the winter."
> —*Barrie Murdock,*
> *cat and plant lover*

Don't

✗ Place houseplants on or near the floor, where they're
   more likely to be nibbled or played with by pets and
   young children.
✗ Buy anything lethal, like datura. It isn't worth the risk.
✗ Grow castor bean plants indoors. They should be
   restricted to the garden.
✗ Get too hung up on the issue of "bad" houseplants.
   Severe poisoning is very rare.

Don't point fingers at poinsettias

People insist that the "Christmas plant" is toxic, causing
everything from tummy upsets to convulsions to death. In
fact, some worry warts refuse to have it in their homes over

the holidays on the grounds that it may make somebody ill. Experts say that's hogwash. Poinsettias are *not* poisonous. Period. They were once thought to be mildly toxic, but both the American and Canadian governments have concluded that they goofed on this point, and they recently crossed the pretty, harmless poinsettia off their poisonous plant lists.

However, since this much-maligned plant is a member of the rash-inducing euphorbia family, it may be wise to wear gloves when handling it.

Which plants absorb pollutants?

Astronauts whirling around in space on shuttle flights for NASA have conducted complex experiments on many common houseplants. Their primary interest was in testing the plants' capacity to purify air, but they made some other amazing findings. Houseplants are, in fact, true friends to humanity. They not only convert carbon dioxide to oxygen, but some of them also have the ability to trap and absorb many of the chemical pollutants that we introduce into our homes. These harmful substances include:

- formaldehyde emitted from foam insulation and soft furnishings (like padded sofas and armchairs);
- trichlorethylene from paints and glues; and
- benzene, found in tobacco smoke and some detergents.

NASA says certain plants are particularly beneficial to have around because they swallow up the bad stuff and regurgitate it as nice clean air. They recommend these:

- Aloe vera (*Aloe barbadensis*)
- Chinese evergreen (*Aglaonema*)
- Chrysanthemum (garden mums, sold as potted plants every fall)
- Dieffenbachia
- English ivy (*Hedera helix*)
- Golden pothos (*Epipremnum aureum*)

- Ficus
- Gerbera daisy
- Philodendron, especially the heart-leaf and lace tree varieties
- *Spathiphyllum* 'Mauna Loa'
- Spider plant (*Chlorophytum comosum*)

The astronauts found that aloes, epipremnums, and philodendrons were particularly good at removing formaldehyde from the air. Gerbera daisies and chrysanthemums worked similar magic with benzene.

> **Hot tip**
>
> "Don't grow miniature roses (*Rosa chinensis*) indoors if you have a cat. Mine loves nibbling on the rose buds. They haven't poisoned her, but it sure wrecks the roses."
>
> —*Joan Thomas, condo gardener*

Where To Get Help for Unhappy Houseplants

It's the middle of the winter, it's well below freezing outside, and suddenly your ficus has dropped all its leaves. What to do? You have several options:

Your friendly neighborhood florist

Establish a relationship with a local business that sells plants—it's worth it. When you have a problem, you can drop by and get their advice, which they are usually only too happy to supply. Many gardeners follow the "cheapest is best" formula: they stick to buying plants from big box stores out in the suburbs. This is certainly cheaper, but savvy souls buy from a local supplier—a florist, garden center, or even a neighborhood greengrocer (these folks are often surprisingly knowledgeable), because when things go wrong, there's a real live person close at hand to quiz about solutions.

Surf the Web

Use a search engine like Google, type in a few words such as "ficus houseplant care," and you'll find links to lots of Web sites related to that topic. Some of the information these sites supply is useful. A lot isn't. Many are created by companies selling products, and there's a ton of marketing hype to wade through before you get to the nitty-gritty stuff you need. Others are written badly, and the type is so small it's hard to read. If you're a techie, you can certainly track down valuable tips—there's so much information floating around in cyber-space nowadays—but if you want fast results, try these first:

❀ **Web sites operated by universities:** Many dispense solid information aimed at gardeners—and while the writing is often dry and academic, you can pick up useful tips. Two good ones are:

  ❀ **http://eesc.orst.edu:** Operated by an organization with a mouthful of a name (Oregon State University Extension and Experiment Station Communications), this has an excellent site on houseplant care.

  ❀ **www.extension.umn.edu/info:** The University of Minnesota manages this one. It's strong on informa-tion about seed-starting.

  ❀ **http://rhs.org.uk/advice:** This is the site of the Royal Horticultural Society in London, England. It's laid out well, is easy to read, and contains useful infor-mation for indoor gardeners.

❀ **www.windowbox.com:** Down-to-earth gardening tips, supplied in a punchy style. Their houseplant expert is called the "Care Counselor," and you can leave your own tips at the site or pick up suggestions from other site users.

❀ **www.chestnut-sw.com:** This site, belonging to an outfit called the Weekend Gardener, offers advice on indoor plant care and starting seeds.

❀ **www.bulb.com:** Operated by the Netherlands Flower Bulb Information Center / USA, this super site has every-thing you need to know about growing all kinds of bulbs.

Ask a Master Gardener

Master Gardeners are trained volunteers who take courses in horticulture. They spend much of their spare time educating the public about gardening, simply because they love it so much. Many of them are houseplant addicts—and they're a mine of information about the pleasures and pitfalls of indoor gardening.

You can find Master Gardeners in information booths at flower shows and agricultural shows. In many cities, they also run gardening information phone lines, which provide free answers to questions about all aspects of growing things. Some MG groups operate advice clinics (usually during the summer months) at garden centers. You can take an ailing houseplant there and get some advice on the spot.

To find out if there's a Master Gardener group operating in your area, ask at your local horticultural society or garden center. Universities that offer agricultural or horticultural programs also know how to track down these knowledgeable and helpful individuals.

Get to know other gardeners

Join your local horticultural society. Local garden centers can usually find phone numbers and addresses for you. If you live in a condo or apartment building, get a gardening group going. In a high-rise, there are bound to be other people already growing things indoors—and they're often a treasure trove of information.

Acknowledgments

There are two things I love about gardening: plants (of course) and people. I've met so many delightful gardeners, from all walks of life. Whatever their particular passion in the great green world, they're always enthusiastic, knowledgeable, and fun to be around. When I get together with other gardeners, there's never a lull in the conversation. We find so many things to talk about! Indeed, it never ceases to amaze me how open-hearted gardeners are. There can be no other group of people who share their creative ideas, practical know-how, and the fruits of their labors (all those plants) so generously.

Many gardeners have assisted me in the preparation of this book. In particular, I want to thank: Janet Brothers, who gave me a lesson in transplanting seedlings at Cedar Springs Nursery in Elora, Ontario; Carol Cowan, of the Netherlands Flower Bulb Information Centre, who shares my passion for growing amaryllis; horticulturist Cathie Cox, who taught me everything I know about starting plants from seed; Mary-Fran McQuade, for her budget-minded savvy with houseplants; African violet aficionado Sandy Morgan; Conrad Richter, a repository of many fascinating facts about herbs; Richard Tawton, who claims to be a beginner with houseplants but is really a pro; indoor gardener extraordinaire Ida Weippert, who appears on the cover; and Paul Zammit, who introduced me to the charms of clivias.

I am also grateful for tips, ideas, and information gleaned from many other sources. One valuable reference guide I recommend for its in-depth information is *Success with House*

Plants, published by Reader's Digest. Another is *From Seed to Bloom*, by Eileen Powell. Two garden writers from whom I gained insights into the pleasures of amaryllis are Starr Ockenga, author of *Amaryllis*, and Veronica Read, author of a book on amaryllis to be published in 2004. Derek Read, of the Research Branch of the Biological Resources Program of Agriculture and Agrifood Canada, provided useful information on poisonous houseplants and the NASA research into beneficial plants. Other tips came from many friends and acquaintances, including: Trevor Ashbee, Deirdre Black, Dugald Cameron, Mark Cullen, Irene Day, Charlie Dobbin, David Eddy, Gwen Farrow, Marianne Fenner, Stewart Hamilton, Becky Heath, Sandra Henry, Lorraine Hunter, Alison Hunberstone, Sara Katz, Priscilla Leung, Anne Lockley, Douglas Markoff, Sue Martin, Barrie Murdock, Truc Nguyen, Catherine Pitt, Andrew Pepetone, Larry Sherk, Joan Thomas, Ann Travis, Mary Wilkerson, Karen York, and Tilly Zomer.

Finally, I wish to thank my editor, Sue Sumeraj, for her expertise in assembling this package of material into a readable (and, I hope, useful) book.

Index